LEARNING TO LEAD

LEARNING TO LEAD

Gaines S. Dobbins

BROADMAN PRESS
Nashville, Tennessee

Dewey Decimal classification number: 158
Library of Congress catalog card number: 68-12342
Printed in the United States of America
5.AT676

To
my students around the world
who exemplify the principle
of leadership as servantship

Preface

Many times I have led survey studies of churches with a view to improvement of their processes and products. To pastor, staff members, deacons, church officers, heads of organizations, and representative workers, I have posed the question: What, in your opinion, is the church's greatest need? The answers varied—from deepened consecration to better building and equipment but invariably concentrated on consecrated, competent, conscientious leadership.

On occasion I have met with a group of interested citizens and asked the same question concerning community need. Again the answers varied—from greater patriotism to a new schoolhouse. Then the question became: What need underlies all these needs and must first be met if the other needs are supplied? Almost invariably the reply was: Willing, dependable, responsible *leadership*. Good leaders will attract loyal followers and together they can do whatever needs to be done.

This book is addressed primarily to churches in need of more and better leaders, but also to communities, institutions, enterprises. It is a book more of principles than methods, although efficient ways of leading are indicated. Its basic assumption is that in almost every church, or other organization, there are present and prospective leaders sufficient to insure success. But these must be discovered, enlisted, motivated, developed, and guided.

Prior conditions to adequate leadership are: realization of the critical need; understanding of the meaning and nature of Christian leadership; clarification of essential qualifications; provision of an adequate plan of training; agreement as to aims and methods; willingness to try out new ways of learning to lead; and a consciousness of the costs and assurance of the rewards.

How, in some measure, to fulfil these conditions is the objective of these studies.

The author gratefully acknowledges his indebtedness to countless students who have studied with him the course in leadership in seminary classes; a host of denominational leaders with whom he has happily served; and the multitude of church workers he has been privileged to guide in leadership conferences at home and overseas. He is also grateful to publishers for permission to quote copyrighted materials, and to Thomas Nelson and Sons for use of the Revised Standard Version of the Bible for Scripture references. The bits of poetry are taken from *Masterpieces of Religious Verse*, edited by James Dalton Morrison, Harper and Brothers, publishers, and are used by permission.

Contents

1 You Can Learn to Lead ● 13

2 The Christian Distinctive ● 27

3 Essential Qualifications ● 40

4 Progress Through Planned Preparation ● 54

5 The Job, the Objectives, the Methods ● 67

6 Achievement Through Teamwork ● 79

7 Changed Ways for Changing Times ● 92

8 The Costs and the Rewards ● 104

A Self-Rating Scale for Leaders ● 119

Reading for Further Enrichment ● 125

LEARNING TO LEAD

1 You Can Learn to Lead

This book is about you—your leadership capacity and responsibility, the urgent need of your service, your preparation and qualification for leadership, your concept of the meaning of Christian leadership, your motives and methods, your resources of equipment and improvement, your relation to fellow workers, your ever-broadening horizons, the costs and rewards of faithful leadership.

Some Basic Assumptions

It is assumed that you are a Christian and a church member; that your baptism symbolized your entrance into a new life in Christ; that you committed yourself to believe what he taught and to obey what he commanded; and that you earnestly desire to make your life count in the fellowship of service with like-minded Christians.

It is further assumed that you can continue to learn to the end of life. Age and circumstances may limit your formal schooling but not your education. You can learn! The evidence is too abundant for the assertion to need argument. There are those who cannot learn, but you are not one of them; otherwise you would not be reading these lines.

It is also assumed that you want to know more about the

what, the why, and the how of leadership—the leadership tasks in the church and beyond; how these tasks are to be performed; and why you should respond to the call to prepare for or accept now a position of leadership responsibility.

It is assumed that studying about leadership will not suffice, apart from experience under guidance. The guidelines proposed in this study are intended to be applied in actual situations. Tests are therefore suggested for determining attitudes, activities, and outcomes as you and your fellow workers seek with Christ to build a church equal to the demands made upon it in today's difficult world.

It is assumed that leaders are both born and made. There are qualities genetically and socially inherited that incline some persons toward leadership more than others. You will do well to examine and assess this inheritance. Then there are qualities to be acquired through processes of learning and experience. These processes you need to understand and practice. Preparation for and effectiveness in leadership make demands that you need to realize and carefully weigh. These requirements must in some measure be met. Just as there is no "royal road to learning," there is no easy path to Christian leadership. The price must be paid if the rewards are to be claimed.

You Can Learn to Lead—and to Lead Better

You are indeed "fearfully and wonderfully made." Of all the billions of persons that have lived, that are now living, and that will live, not one ever was or ever will be exactly like you. Your biological inheritance goes back in an unbroken line to the first man and woman created in the divine image. Your characteristics are a mixture in decreasing ratio from immediate parents to remote ancestors. As a human being, you represent the crown of God's creation.

In addition to your biological inheritance, you possess a vast social heritage. You were born in a given community and therefore immediately influenced by its ways of life. You came from a racial stock and necessarily adopted its language, traditions, attitudes, and viewpoints. You became a citizen of a nation and consequently assumed certain responsibilities and accepted certain privileges.

You were educated in schools not of your own choosing, by teachers who, consciously and unconsciously, influenced you. You grew to maturity in a political, cultural, and economic environment that shaped you more than you helped to shape. Your religious beliefs and practices you have acquired, in large measure, from parents, teachers, pastors, companions, books. "I am a part of all that I have met" is not poetic fancy but literal truth.

You were endowed with the greatest faculty bestowed on any of God's creatures—moral choice. True, you were shaped by birth and environment; but at every turn since the age of accountability you have made decisions for which you were responsible. You decided whether to use or abuse your inherited physical powers; you decided whether to be a credit or discredit to your family and society; you decided whether to claim or waste your educational opportunities; you decided whether to be a worthy or unworthy citizen; you decided whether to turn from sin and follow Jesus Christ or to cling to sin and reject the Saviour.

Since your decisions have in the main been in the right direction, you must decide what kind of Christian and church member you will be—active or inactive, a lifter or a leaner, a leader or a camp follower. Standing at attention, you ask: "Lord, what will you have me to do? With your help, I can do your bidding."

The little word "can" means to be able—physically, mentally, socially, legally, morally, and spiritually. It means to possess the qualities and qualifications necessary for the accomplishment of desired purposes or ends. It says that inherited potentialities may be translated into actualities. It asserts that you can be what you want to be and have what you want to have if you meet the conditions.

When you say, "I can," you mobilize powers of which you may not even be aware. It is said that the typical person does not develop and utilize more than one-tenth of his latent abilities. Why could you not eventually become proficient as a painter, musician, sculptor, architect, scientist, writer, doctor, lawyer, industrialist, engineer, or any of a score of occupations? For one thing, there is not time enough; to excel in any one field exhausts the limits of the average life. But you might, given time and determination.

When you say, "I can and I will be the best possible leader for Christ," you not only release powers that aid you to become your best in other directions but you tap divine resources that bring out the best in you as a person.

When you say, "I can!" you accept your partnership with Christ and your fellow Christians.

You can learn.—You began to learn when you were born and you have been learning ever since. The words "can" and "know" are closely related—"can," to be able, and "ken," to know. Knowing and doing are correlatives, each being dependent on the other. Animals have a limited, instinctive capacity to learn; but man's learning is vastly greater, both in amount and kind. It is claimed for the mechanical brain that it can learn, but it is also said that for such a machine to match the human brain it would have to be bigger than the Empire State Building and complex beyond imagination.

How we learn is the subject of much modern investigation. Learning involves three major factors: an amazing receiving and responding system; situations of stimulation; and human association and guidance. Given right conditions, the potential of human learning is limitless. While astronauts are exploring outer space, psychologists are exploring the inner world of consciousness. Both come up with the same answer: You can learn; to which they add, You must keep on learning if you are to survive. The kind and quality of your learning—and that of others like you—will determine the future of the human race.

Leadership is one of the finest and most necessary of human capabilities; it is an art to be learned.

Ordway Tead's *The Art of Leadership* describes the leader as "an artist—an artist working in a medium which is at once complex and universal. His material is people. And just as the task of the artist is one of organization of ideas or materials if any work of art is to be achieved, so with leadership, the bringing of human desires and energy into organized relations becomes a work of high artistry" (p. 33).

Artists may by nature be equipped with certain qualities that help, but this does not take the place of enthusiasm, dedication, practice, work. To lead requires knowledge of the process, acquaintance with the field, understanding and love of people, skill in operation, and sustaining motive. To lead successfully demands that these requirements be met. These are conditions that you can fulfil. Therefore, you can learn to lead!

You Need a Clear Concept of Leadership

Leadership needs more careful definition. There are many popular misconceptions. The leader may be thought of as the man with the biggest and most powerful car, and who keeps ahead of the slower procession. Or the leader may be thought of as the "big chief" who sits at his mahogany desk surrounded by secretaries and assistants. Or the leader may be thought of as the man in command of an army or corporation or institution, who can "say to one, 'Go,' and he goes, and to another, 'Come,' and he comes, and to my slave, 'Do this,' and he does it" (Matt. 8:9). Or the image of the leader may be that of the popular and powerful champion of a cause who can rally followers to his support. Or the concept may be that of the genius who by his outstanding ability is recognized as the first in his field. Sometimes the leader is one who is accepted and followed because he promises to gain for his adherents the advantages which they seek for themselves. Common to all of these concepts of leadership is the idea of dominance, superiority, command, and control of others. This is not the kind of leadership needed in your church. You are needed to serve, not to be served.

You Are Needed to Lead

Suppose the church council met—pastor, staff, church officers, representatives of the various church organizations—and the question to be discussed was: *What is our greatest single need?* The answers would no doubt vary: deepened consecration; enlarged outreach for the unreached; improved methods; more building space and better facilities; increased financial support; greater evangelistic and missionary effectiveness; more concern for personal, family, and community needs.

Suppose the question then became: *What are the broader needs, beyond the church itself* (including community, state, nation, world, denomination)? Again the replies would be varied: better homes and schools, higher moral standards, improved race relations, better economic conditions, better government, better use of modern technology, peace and goodwill among the nations, denominational unity, and missionary advance.

Is there not an underlying question that must be answered before any of these needs can be effectually met? What is the need which if unmet makes improbable the solution to any of these problems? Almost unanimously will come the reply: capable, dependable, responsible *leadership!* Such leadership— in the right direction, with unselfish motives, and for agreed ends—will attract intelligent and loyal followers who can eventually do whatever needs to be done. Without such leaders and followers, any enterprise is doomed to eventual failure. With such leaders and followers, success is ultimately assured.

The unfortunate situation is that in today's world such leadership is, in the language of business, in short supply. This is true in the church, in the state, in business, in industry, in the professions, and in organized society as a whole. The shortage is made all the more unfortunate by the increasing complexity of life, the unprecedented growth of population, the congestion and disintergration of cities, the increasing incidence of immorality and crime, and the antagonisms that threaten the peace of communities, nations, the world.

Whence will come the supply of the urgently needed leadership? Can we safely look to the mass media of communication, the schools, political parties, social and industrial organizations, the learned professions, philanthropic societies? Each of these may have a share, but the one institution adequate for the task is the church of Jesus Christ, functioning according to New Testament principles and patterns. Do you see yourself in the picture? *You* are needed to lead!

You are needed to lead in Christian action.—Jesus Christ is where the action is. He never intended that his worship and service should be confined to the walls of a building. During his ministry, he preached and taught and wrought more often on the streets, in the marketplace, on a hillside, or at the seaside, than in the Temple or synagogue. Indeed, he repudiated the narrow institutionalism of the religious leaders.

Paul embodied the spirit of his Master as he bore his witness in the heat of intense opposition and controversy.

The church is not a sociopolitical institution nor a business enterprise. But it does have the responsibility of permeating all social and economic relations with Christian principles. The church may not accomplish this best through direct action; but it can, through its members, effectually direct the action. Such direction will be in the spirit of love, even for enemies. Yet, love can at times be as frank and severe as was Jesus in his denunciation of the Pharisees.

There is a "wall of separation" between church and state, but this does not mean that they are wholly separate each from the other. There should be a door in the wall through which religion and politics can pass back and forth in free and helpful communication.

Politicians are better servants of the people if they are Christians; and Christians may be better servants of Christ and his church if they engage honorably and wisely in politics. This is true in business, the professions, and other human affairs as well.

The training which church members get in Christian leadership should carry over into practice in all other areas of service. You are needed to give leadership in situations calling for action in Christ's name and for his sake.

You are needed to help replace bad leadership with good.— Never doubt it—there will be leadership, good or bad. There has been before and there is now altogether too much bad leadership. Leaders that lead in the wrong direction are to be found in religion, politics, industry, education, the professions, the communications media, entertainment, sports—wherever you look.

Many Christians decry this unfortunate situation, yet refuse to seek or accept leadership responsibility. They excuse themselves on the grounds that they are too busy, or that they don't want to get involved, or that they don't have aptitude or inclination, or that someone else can do the job better. They are like the men in the parable who were invited to the feast; they invented flimsy excuses for not doing what they really didn't want to do. They got out of going to the feast, but they shut the door of opportunity in their faces forever.

The consequences of bad leadership are far-reaching and inescapable. The argument, "It's none of my business," is fallacious. The riot led by racial extremists may destroy your own property. The political demagogue who gains power may bankrupt your business. The troublemaker in the church may sow discord that will alienate your children from Christ. Even on the level of self-interest, you cannot afford to shirk responsibility for bad leadership.

On the higher level of loyalty to Christ and the welfare of others, bad leadership must be replaced by good. The church, the school, the community, the nation, and the whole world suffer when the wrong men are in command. When Pharaoh stubbornly refused to let the Chosen People go, plagues came upon all Egypt. When kings of Israel "did that which was evil in the sight of the Lord," the whole nation suffered. Wars, ancient and modern, have devastated the land because of misguided ambition on the part of evil rulers.

Current history records exploitation of the weak by the strong. Hide as we may, we cannot escape the fact that we are our brothers' keepers. The only way to get rid of the wrong kind of leadership is to replace it with the right kind. Your help to make the replacement is urgently needed.

Edmund Burke, an English statesman, said it two centuries

ago: "All that is necessary for the triumph of evil in the world is that good men do nothing."

You are needed to lead in your church.—A church at its best is a spiritual democracy. Democracy stands for more than the right to elect officeholders. A democracy holds that the right to participate involves the duty to participate. In a democracy, the rulers are the ruled. A church after the New Testament fashion cannot delegate authority to an "inner circle" and thus absolve the members from leadership responsibility.

Leadership in a democracy is essentially a matter of initiative —seeing and doing what needs to be done. Election to office does not automatically make one a leader. Not to be so elected does not relieve one from leadership obligation. In the Jerusalem church, the apostles took the lead by reason of their appointment by Jesus. But "the company of those who believed were of one heart and soul" (Acts 4:32). They bore witness individually and collectively.

Your church needs your leadership because it is thus that you grow to Christian maturity. Wise parents know that responsibility must pass from them to the child if the child is to be prepared for the duties of mature life. The oversheltered child becomes the spoiled man or woman. You are in danger of becoming a "spoiled" church member if you passively accept direction and never learn to act on your own. The gravest mistake is to take no active part in the life and work of your church, even though in doing so you sometimes make a mistake!

Your church needs your leadership because thus it builds a vital fellowship. A synonym for *fellowship* is partnership. A partner is one who shares in activity with another. He may be a "silent partner," in which case he is involved for what he can get, not for what he can contribute of himself. A church made up principally of "silent partners" may have a budget but it will not be a brotherhood. Just as there is no such thing as proxy salvation, so there can be no proxy participation.

Church fellowship is not automatic—it must be developed in a community of shared faith and works. To the extent that you and others feel no sense of leadership responsibility, the church is weakened. You are needed that your church may be a true *koinonia*, a Christian community.

You Need to Be Concerned

The word "lost" takes on more and more terrible meaning as population increases and the threat of world destruction grows more ominous. Consider the millions of lives and billions of dollars lost in the two recent World Wars—the most destructive in history. Consider what is being lost now in manpower and taxes to pay expenses of past and present wars. Consider what is lost through crime, ignorance, idleness, immorality, exploitation, poverty, negligence. Consider the lost happiness brought about by broken homes and wasted lives. Consider the grim prospect of increased lostness in all these and other areas in the years ahead. If the course continues, civilization itself may be lost.

In the church itself, among its own members, the word "lost" has a dark and tragic meaning. Canvass the church roll to discover how many members have been lost, their addresses unknown, their church relationship vanished. If your church is typical, the number will be about one-third of the total membership. Continue to study to determine how many resident members are almost entirely inactive, attending services rarely if at all, giving nothing, rendering no service, bearing no witness. Granting that their souls are saved if they once truly trusted Christ, evidently, for the time, their usefulness to Christ and his church is lost. Here is lostness that must grieve the heart of

God. Perhaps this backsliding is not altogether their fault. The church, for lack of concerned leadership, may bear a part of the blame. You are needed to conserve them for Christ.

To be lost in the biblical sense means to be forever alienated from God and all that is good. This is a lostness infinitely more terrible than anything conceivable on the human plane. The word Jesus used for hell is translated from *gehenna,* a place near Jerusalem where filth was burned.

To be "cast into hell" is to be forever shut out from heaven, to live eternally in the remorse of unforgiven sin. It is said that in a theology class taught by Dr. W. T. Conner of Southwestern Baptist Theological Seminary, a student used the word "hell" flippantly. The professor stood silent, then walked to the nearby window and gazed out, as if in pain. Then he turned to the hushed class and said, "Never use that word lightly. Men are going there."

In fact, many are already there even before they die—living on the garbage heap of life when they might be feasting on heavenly manna. Their fault? Perhaps not altogether—maybe no one ever sought to lead them to Christ. The prophet puts it vividly: "If the watchman sees the sword coming and does not blow the trumpet . . . and the sword comes, and takes any one of them; that man is taken away in his iniquity, but his blood I will require at the watchman's hand" (Ezek. 33:6).

You are needed and commissioned to lead the lost to the Saviour, "to open their eyes, that they may turn from darkness to light and from the power of Satan to God, that they may receive forgiveness of sins and a place among those who are sanctified by faith in me" (Acts 26:18).

Things happen when Christians get deeply concerned. It is doubtful if we do much earnest praying unless our hearts are burdened. The burden of leadership need must first be felt.

Are you troubled because you do not have a significant part in the work of your church? Does your conscience sometimes hurt because, having a church responsibility, you take it rather lightly? Do you fully realize how the cause of Christ suffers and your church is weakened if you shrug off these questions and do nothing about the need?

The burden of leadership need may not be so much that of personal dereliction as indifference to the shortage of leadership supply. Even though you are doing your part reasonably well, you may be like the soldier on the firing line who is crippled and endangered if reinforcements are not supplied.

Your church is engaged in the most crucial of all battles—the struggle for the minds and souls of men. To lose this fight is eventually to lose all else. This Christian warfare is one in which "we are not contending against flesh and blood, but against the principalities, against the powers, against the world rulers of this present darkness, against the spiritual hosts of wickedness in the heavenly places," writes Paul, as if speaking to the present situation. He then sounds the stirring call: "Therefore take the whole armor of God, that you may be able to withstand in the evil day, and having done all, to stand. . . . Take the helmet of salvation, and the sword of the Spirit, which is the word of God" and launch the attack! (Eph. 6:12-17).

Every soldier in this mighty spiritual warfare is both a leader and a follower—a leader in the fight and a follower of Jesus Christ. You are not worthy to be enlisted unless, like him, you are deeply concerned. Ethelwyn Weatherald has put it into verse:

> My orders are to fight;
>   Then if I bleed or fail,
> Or strongly win, what matters it?
>   God only doth prevail.

> The servant craveth naught
> Except to serve with might.
> I was not told to win or lose,—
> My orders are to fight!

Something to Think and Pray About

Did you grow up with the idea that the leader is an exceptional person, by reason of birth, office, achievement, genius? If so, have you outgrown it?

What assumptions about you indicate your actual or potential fitness for leadership?

What are implications for your possibilities of leadership in the statement, "You can learn to lead"?

What conditions in and out of the church point to the urgent demand for more and better leadership?

Why does the need for leadership underlie all other needs?

What are some fields, beyond the church, that call urgently for Christian leadership?

What happens if Christians excuse themselves and evil forces take over leadership?

For what purpose does your church immediately and urgently need your responsible service?

Why should you concern yourself with this need?

2 The Christian Distinctive

The distinguishing mark of the leader, in the traditional popular concept, may take one of several forms. The image will vary with time and circumstance and the history and culture of the people.

Popular Images of the Leader

Historically, the image of the leader most generally held has been that of the exceptional man endued with the power to command. We think at once of kings, emperors, generals, popes, bishops, presidents, governors, capitalists, labor leaders, and the like. Their office invests them with authority and their leadership is chiefly that of official position.

Another image of the leader is that of the activist. He wins the right to be a leader because he gets things done. He sees a need and proceeds to organize resources to meet it. The need may be material—better living conditions, especially for the underprivileged. The need may be social—better relations among persons, with freedom and justice for all. The need may be moral—the cleaning up of conditions that make for delinquency, immorality, crime. The need may be educational—more and better schools and greater equality of educational opportunity. Or, the need may be spiritual—breaking down barriers of

27

alienation and sin and increasing love of God and neighbor. Men who want action turn to such an activist as their leader and become his followers and supporters.

Another image of the leader is that of the man of superior intelligence and originality. He is accepted as a leader in the field of ideas. In this field of leadership, we think of the philosophers, theologians, poets, novelists and dramatists, scientists and inventors, originators of new ways of thinking and believing. Not always are their ideas acceptable at first and frequently they are persecuted. Yet ultimately, if not immediately, they win a following and are placed in the hall of fame as leaders of thought. Sometimes the heretic of yesterday becomes the orthodox thinker of tomorrow, and the innovator today may be later rejected by his more thoughtful successors.

The image of the leader may be that of the idealist. The function of the idealist is to improve on reality. He sees what others see, but he sees more. Beyond ugliness he sees beauty, beyond evil he sees good, beyond falsehood he sees truth. He may communicate his insight through literature, music, painting, architecture, oratory—by whatever art form his artistry seeks expression. He combines insight with skill so that his mastery becomes evident to the viewer or hearer. In time, what he produces is recognized as "classical," that is, of the first class. He may even become the founder of a "school" of followers who accept his ideals and undertake to imitate and perpetuate them.

The image of a leader may be that of the man who is outstanding in the spiritual realm. His concern is for the things of the spirit, the unseen values of life, the relationships of the human and the divine. In this category may be placed the founders of the great ethnic religions: Buddha, Confucius, Lao Tze, Muhammad.

When we think of spiritual leaders, we include the Old

Testament patriarchs: Moses, Samuel, David, the seers and prophets of Israel. Supremely, we head the list of idealists with Jesus Christ and follow his name with the apostles, especially Paul. The list then becomes a long one of leaders of the spirit in Christian history, from the first century to the present. They are remembered because they sought to make men hear and follow the call of the Lord.

What do these popular, traditional images of the leader disclose? In general, five things: That he (or she) (1) is an exceptional person; (2) possesses elements of authority (3) has unusual ability and mastery (4) exhibits traits of personality that gain attention; and (5) exercises influence over others that makes them voluntary or involuntary followers.

Quite often, if not always, several of these characteristics are combined in the same person, although one quality is usually predominant. Generally, the leader is accepted because he helps his followers to get what they want or to be what they desire. The measure of his greatness is in terms of his successful achievements or his personal accomplishments or both. Such a leader stands out from ordinary men and women as extraordinary, to be followed because, in his position or in his field, he is ahead of the crowd.

Christianity's Revolutionary Concept

There is realistic recognition that there are and have always been exceptional persons who have exercised leadership, some to bless and others to curse their followers. But the concept that the only leaders are exceptional persons, who are unusually powerful or prominent, is sharply challenged by Christianity.

Jesus Christ revealed the true distinctive of Christian leadership. He gathered about him a group of ordinary men from the ordinary walks of life. They held no office; they were not notable men of action; they were not conspicuous for their ideas or ideals; they were not men of religious power or influence. They were evidently men of good sense and character, open-minded and teachable, who were convinced of the claims of Christ and so became his disciples. After a night of prayer, which Jesus no doubt spent in conversation with his Father about the qualifications and potentialities of these select men, he appointed twelve "to be with him, and to be sent out to preach and have authority to cast out demons" (Mark 3:14-15). As they accompanied him, they caught his spirit, learned his message, understood his redemptive mission, and observed and imitated his method. They left their work and gave full time to this discipleship.

Soon we see something happening to these erstwhile ordinary men. They discovered that they had powers of which they had not been aware. They caught a vision of the restoration of the kingdom to Israel, with themselves holding the most important positions. Evidently they became ambitious to be leaders after the fashion of the world.

James and John, encouraged by their mother, approached Jesus secretly to request of him the two most important places in his coming kingdom—one on his right hand, the other on his left. Rebuking them, Jesus pointed out that he could not show favoritism; besides, it was not his to decide but the Heavenly Father's. Somehow the other ten men learned of this trickery and were angry. A quarrel arose among them as to who then should be the greatest.

This break in the fellowship of the twelve over ambition for leadership provided Jesus the occasion to set forth the radical distinctive of Christian leadership. He pointed to the pyramidal structure of the government under which they lived—the emperor at the top and other rulers in descending order. "It shall not be so among you," he said. "But whoever would be great among you must be your servant, and whoever would be first among you must be your slave." Then he gave himself as the example: "Even as the Son of man came not to be served but to serve, and to give his life as a ransom for many" (Matt. 20:26-28).

Here then is the Christian distinctive: leadership is not getting above others in prestige and power. It is servantship—getting down under the load of human need to bear it sacrificially and redemptively. According to this standard, the measure of greatness is not prominence but humility, not excellence but faithfulness, not authority but obedience, not being served but service. Eventually these men and their successors learned that leadership is servantship.

This radical concept of leadership carries with it far-reaching implications, especially for the solution of a church's leadership problems.

Implications for the Church

Exceptional persons may be found in every community.—They may hold public office or they may be outstanding in fields of action, thought, ideals, religion. If they are not Christian, they should be earnestly sought for Christ; if nominally Christian but inactive in the church, they should be enlisted in its service. Such key persons can unlock many doors for the church that otherwise remain closed. Moses in the Old Testament, Paul in the New are examples of God's mighty use of strategic men.

In the membership of almost every church there are potential leaders who are being overlooked.—They perhaps have never thought of themselves as occupying positions of responsibility; the church has probably assumed that they cannot or will not serve. Yet if prayerfully approached and challenged, they may yield their lives, talents, and services to Christ and his church.

The basic qualification for Christian leadership is full accep-
tance of the concept of Jesus Christ that leadership is servant-
ship.—This is the Christian distinctive. If it is missed, trouble
lies ahead. Many, if not most, church ruptures can be traced
directly or indirectly to failure to recognize and practice this
distinctive.

Historic Violations of This Distinctive

Early in Christian history the struggle for preeminence began.
As Christianity grew and spread, large churches developed in the
principal cities of Europe and Asia Minor. Metropolitan pastors
became "bishops" and assumed authority over their dioceses.
Because of their position, they gained authority over lesser
pastors. By the close of the fifth century, five metropolitan
centers or "patriarchates" were recognized: Rome, Antioch, Alex-
andria, Constantinople, and Jerusalem. In the struggle for first
place, Rome won out; and the bishop of Rome became the "papa"
(pope) of Christendom. The ambition for power—inherent in
men—found expression in the increasingly extravagant claims of
the bishops or popes of Rome. After the fall of Rome (A.D. 410)
chaos ensued over much of the Empire. The once powerful
Roman legions were powerless against the barbarian invaders.
Awed by the claims and rituals of the priests, many of the
barbarian chiefs submitted to baptism and in turn compelled
their people to be baptized.

Thus the church came to wield much of the power formerly
belonging to the emperor and the Roman *curia* or senate. The
pope assumed the title *Pontifex Maximus* (Keeper of the Bridge),
by which the emperor had been known. He claimed to be the
successor of Peter, the vicar (proxy) of Jesus Christ, the Holy
Father, the supreme ruler of the church on earth. Next to
him were the cardinals; next to them, the archbishops and

bishops; then, in descending order, various classes of priests. Underneath all these were the people, supporting and obeying the hierarchy. The pyramid of Jesus had been reversed—the great man was the one being served; the little man the one who served.

There were reformers before the Reformation, but the sixteenth century witnessed a more or less successful revolt against the authoritarian system of the Roman Church. The reformed churches corrected many abuses in matters of doctrine and practice, but only partially did they rid themselves of the secular concept of leadership. "Orders of the ministry" were largely retained. Bishops were put in charge of territorial churches and maintained a measure of control over congregations and pastors; and the pastors often in turn exercised authority over their charges and local officers. It has never been easy to eradicate this deep-seated concept of leadership as conferring the right to command.

Efforts to Reestablish the Distinctive

The democratic movement swept over Europe in the seventeenth and eighteenth centuries and moved westward to the New World. Its basic proposition was that men have the right to be free and to rule themselves. The revolution was resisted by hierarchical and episcopal type churches, but was approved and promoted by churches of the congregational order. In varying degrees and with differing measures of success these church bodies sought to place authority and responsibility in the hands of the congregation. In principle, each church would possess the right to manage its own affairs and select its own leaders. Ideally, this right extended to every qualified member of the congregation.

Separation between "clergy" and "laity" was theoretically

rejected. The words of Jesus were taken seriously: "Neither be called masters, for you have one master, the Christ. He who is greatest among you shall be your servant; whoever exalts himself will be humbled, and whoever humbles himself will be exalted" (Matt. 23:10-12).

These churches accordingly ordained or gave approval to men believed upon examination to be called of God to the gospel ministry or to the deaconship. Each church called or terminated the services of its pastor and other members of the employed staff. Under committee guidance, the congregation elected to office its leaders of the church and its organizations. When application was made for membership in the body, the congregation voted its approval or disapproval. Such a church took justifiable pride in designating itself as a spiritual democracy. In principle, it undertook to restore the Christian distinctive of leadership as servantship.

Small and few in numbers at the beginning, these churches have grown to be many, and often large and prosperous. Their problems of scarcity have been exchanged for problems of plenty. Their simplicity of organization has largely given way to complexity. The necessity of delegated leadership tends to make congregational control nominal rather than real. The question arises as to whether or not the Christian principle of leadership can survive.

The Christian Distinctive Imperiled

The Christian distinctive of leadership as servantship is endangered by the widespread and absorbing desire for things. Many, if not most, church members yield to some extent to the desire for "better things for better living"—a modern residence with automatic conveniences, an automobile (perhaps two or more), radio and television, gas or electric heat for winter and cooling system for summer. In business and industry, operations once performed by hands are now performed by machines. Certainly this is not wrong in itself, but it tends to discount the idea of personal service.

"In the sweat of your face shall you eat bread" has an unrealistic sound in the ears of today's Adam! If the easier way is taken in all other areas of human endeavor, why not also in the church? Leadership requires expenditure of time and effort, which many have become habituated to avoid.

The Christian leadership distinctive is imperiled by the rush of modern life. Everywhere people are in a hurry. Witness the speed of travel on highways and in the air. Despite the aid of laborsaving and timesaving devices, people's lives are overcrowded as never before. Pressed to take a position of responsibility in the church, their stock reply is, "We haven't the time." Often the leader comes before the group with the lame excuse, "I'm sorry to be unprepared—I just didn't have the time." If the role is truly that of the "servant of Jesus Christ," his service must come first. Otherwise, the Christian distinctive is marred.

The Christian leadership distinctive is jeopardized by self-interest. "What's in it for me?" becomes the usual question in an acquisitive society. Living in such an atmosphere, the Christian is liable to adopt this attitude unconsciously. Church work is not without its rich reward, but if self-interest is the motive, there will be disappointment. In the service of Christ and his church, self-interest must be submerged. Some church members run contrary to this philosophy. When this is true, the Christian principle of leadership is violated.

Other perils to the principle may be suggested—"immorality, impurity, licentiousness, idolatry, sorcery, enmity, strife, jealousy, anger, selfishness, dissension, party spirit, envy, drunkenness, carousing, and the like" (Gal. 5:19-21). Paul's list is a long and ugly one, but it should be remembered that he was writing to warn Christians who may be tempted to produce these "works of the flesh." Assuredly such unworthy church members who fall into sins like these cannot qualify as servants of Jesus Christ and their brethren.

The Christian Distinctive Exemplified

There is a bright side of the picture. From the apostles until now, servant-Christians have achieved notable leadership. We are reminded of the list of "heroes of faith" in Hebrews 11; of scholars like Justin Martyr, who suffered death because of his defense of the gospel; and of the heroic men and women who gave up their lives for Christ's sake during the period of Roman persecution.

The Reformation had its suffering servants such as Wycliffe, Huss, Felix Manz, Latimer, Cranmer, Hubmaier, Luther, Melanchthon, John Knox, and others less notable but no less noble in their self-forgetting service, men who "counted not their lives as dear unto themselves."

Baptists have their full quota of such men—William Carey, Andrew Fuller, Robert Hall, Charles Spurgeon; in America, Roger Williams, John Clark, Obadiah Holmes, John Peck, Adoniram Judson, Luther Rice, Richard Furman, Jesse Mercer, Jeremiah Jeter . . . the list becomes longer as the Baptist cause grows stronger.

Only "the Lamb's Book of Life" will be sufficient to name those down to this day who have exemplified the principle of leadership as servantship.

Look about you and see the principle in practice in your church and community. Think of the pastors and staff members who have served sacrificially; of deacons, church officers, Sunday School officers and teachers, leaders of Training Union, Woman's

Missionary Union, Baptist Men, Music Ministries, and other church activities, who have ungrudgingly given of their time and energy, without thought of pay. Recall men and women in public service whose ambition it was to spend and be spent for the sake of others.

Perhaps most conspicuous in their demonstration of the principle are the missionaries at home and abroad who have lost their lives to find them again in their leadership of the Christian mission. They, more than the politicians and militarists, are capable of leading the world out of its darkness and strife into light and peace.

The Call to Leadership a Call to Servantship

Servantship does not imply a dead level of mediocrity. It does not mean satisfaction with inferiority, surrender of desire for significance, renunciation of hope of high achievement. On the contrary, Christian servantship is the surest way to rightful superiority, the living of a life full of meaning, the realization of high hopes and noble dreams. Christian servantship is the surest guarantee against the emptiness of life to which men who have lived for self and self-centered satisfactions inevitably come.

As Jesus was preparing to leave them, he said to the little band of plain men gathered about him, "Truly, truly, I say to you, he who believes in me will also do the works that I do; and greater works than these will he do" (John 14:12).

He comforted them by promising that he would go to prepare a place for them, that where he was they would be also. He offered them the priceless privilege of prayer, according to which whatever they asked in his name they would obtain. He assured them of the presence and power of the Holy Spirit, to be with them forever.

At this point Judas (not Iscariot) interrupted, as if in amaze-
ment that Jesus should be thus speaking to them—an insignificant
little band of ordinary men. "How is it" he asked, "that you
will manifest yourself to us, and not to the world?" (v. 22).
Why should he not be making these promises and disclosures to
the great and powerful rather than to them, unknown and
inconsequential men?

To this inquiry Jesus made reply: "If a man loves me, he will
keep my word, and my Father will love him, and we will come
to him and make our home with him" (v. 23). That is to say,
no man who believes in and becomes a servant of Jesus Christ
can be ordinary, insignificant, inconsequential! History demon-
strates the truth of Christ's words, for these plain men became
the leaders of the movement that changed the course of the
world. Their names are remembered when the so-called great
of their time have sunk into oblivion.

The promise is to you and to any other Christian who will
meet the condition: "Whoever would be great among you must
be your servant" (Matt. 20:26).

M. Woolsy Stryker prayed:

> Our hearts be ruled, our spirits schooled
> Alone Thy will to seek;
> And when we find Thy blessed mind,
> Instruct our lips to speak.

Something to Think and Pray About

Have I grown up with the concept of the great man as exceptional leader of action, of thought, of ideals, of the spirit? Why?

What do these several concepts of the leader have in common?

What revolutionary concept of leadership did Jesus introduce?
How fully am I prepared to accept it?

If Jesus' concept of the leader were fully accepted, what would it mean (1) for me personally? (2) for the church and community?

How did wrong concepts of leadership arise in early Christianity? What were the consequences?

Wherein did the Reformation fail to recover the Christian distinctive of leadership? To what extent has this failure been carried over into the churches today?

In what ways is the Christian leadership distinctive being imperiled in your church and denomination? In your own life?

What is the bright side of the picture? What examples can you give of leaders who demonstrate the distinctive? Are you resolved to "follow in their train"?

3 Essential Qualifications

Where shall we find the leaders we need? The cry comes from many quarters. There is no question about the demand, but whence the supply? Are leaders a peculiar breed, born with certain capabilities that set them apart; or are they average persons who have developed certain traits and abilities? The question persists, are leaders born or made?

Leadership Qualifications

Those charged with finding and selecting leaders generally have gone on the assumption that they must look for qualities already possessed.

Lists of leadership qualifications usually include physical and mental health; personal attractiveness; above-average intelligence; superior educational background and experience; clearly defined aims; contagious enthusiasm; perseverance in the face of discouragement; ability to learn and willingness to share; good reputation and integrity of character; devotion to the task and loyalty to the cause.

Let us examine each of these and evaluate its necessity for the leader, especially the Christian leader in the church.

Physical health.—Sound physical and mental health is of course highly desirable on the part of anyone who carries responsibility. The New Testament affirms the Greek ideal of "a sound mind in a sound body." Most of the miracles of Jesus were performed to restore the sick-minded to healthy-mindedness, the lame of body to healthy physical function.

Clearly there is a Christian doctrine of health. Paul declares that the body is a member of Christ and the temple of the Holy Spirit (1 Cor. 6:15,19). It is therefore a Christian duty to maintain Christian health at the highest possible level.

The Christian leader especially owes it to Christ, to the church, to those he serves, and to himself to avoid whatever would lower his vitality and to conform faithfully to the rules of sound hygiene.

Suppose, however, the Christian is unfortunately—often unavoidably—handicapped? Will ill health or defective vision or hardness of hearing or lameness or similar disability bar him from some form of leadership? The answer is an emphatic no!

Paul had his "thorn in the flesh." Some of the most useful leaders, in the church and in society, have suffered from disabilities. Often the handicap is a spur to greater achievement. Both because and in spite of the defect, the handicapped Christian may become one of the most useful members of the church and community. With Paul, he says, "Thy grace is sufficient."

Personal attractiveness.—Personal attractiveness is an elusive but highly important quality. Politicians, entertainers, salespersons, and others who seek public favor realize how essential is the indefinable something called "charm." It may be associated with physical attractiveness, social graces, intriguing mannerisms, exceptional ability, masterful attitude, or a combination of these and other qualities that set one apart as distinctive and appealing.

May a Christian be lacking in these elements of personal attractiveness and yet be a magnetic leader? Happily, the answer again is yes. Possessing all of the embellishments but without love, he may be "as sounding brass, or a tinkling cymbal." Filled with a love of Christ that expresses itself in the love of others, the Christian without adornment may yet become one of the most personally attractive of leaders. "Love never fails."

Above-average intelligence.—Intelligence is a prerequisite to success in any human endeavor. Intelligence, however, like personality, is not easily defined. In general, to be intelligent means to be endowed with the faculty of perceiving, knowing, understanding. More technically, intelligence refers to the ability to deal with life situations, to solve problems as they arise, to utilize knowledge purposefully. Obviously there are different levels of intelligence, all the way from the mentally defective to the genius.

The leader is usually thought of as one who possesses above-average intelligence. Leadership, of course, requires at least normal intelligence, but must one be superior in order to lead for Christ? Observation discloses that the Christian with only average mental capacity who consecrates what he has to the service of Christ will be more useful than the brilliant person who lacks such motivation. Intelligence matures with use.

A Christian at first considered unpromising may develop into one of the most useful members of the group. Confidently the humble Christian, called to a place of responsibility, can say, "I can do all things in him who strengthens me" (Phil. 4:13).

Superior educational background and experience.—A favorable background of experience is usually considered essential to leadership in a given field. "What does he know about the job?" is asked concerning a person who is seeking or being sought for a position of responsibility. Acquaintance with any situation by personal observation or practice is of course highly valuable. Yet experience must have a beginning point, prior to which the beginner is of necessity inexperienced. In most trades, the worker must serve an apprenticeship before he is recognized as a full-fledged master workman.

Paul states the principle concerning deacons: "Let them also be tested first; then if they prove themselves blameless let them serve as deacons" (1 Tim. 3:10). Clearly this period of testing must have a starting point from which the prospective leader moves from lesser to great responsibility.

It is unfortunate if the beginner is thrust into a situation which is beyond his ability. But he should not be deprived of the privilege of service on the ground of lack of experience. Obviously no one can gain experience for the difficult task without previous experience in the less difficult.

Clearly defined aims.—The leader needs to know where he is going. Aimless leadership is bound to be poor leadership. But how does one come to have clearly defined aims? Paul gives the formula: "Do your best to present yourself to God as one approved, a workman who has no need to be ashamed, rightly handling the word of truth" (2 Tim. 2:15). Here the high aim is stated as "rightly handling the word of truth"; yet the aim is not realized apart from effort, motivation, end result.

Objectives become clearer as the leader forges ahead, with God's approval and the Bible as his guide.

A clear definition of aims cannot be expected at the beginning of one's Christian service. Clarification is a process, not ordinarily an instantaneous illumination. The beginning leader will get light from a number of sources—observation of others who are doing the same type of work; reading books and articles; instruction from a more experienced person; discussion in a group of fellow workers; observation of the group being led and study of their responses and growth; and prayer.

"If any of you lacks wisdom, let him ask God who gives to all men generously and without reproaching," admonishes the practical apostle (James 1:5). No one can see fully the end from the beginning; aims will change with changing conditions and growing persons. It is therefore impractical to demand of the leader, new or old, a precise and fixed statement of aims.

Contagious enthusiasm.—Enthusiasm is a highly important ingredient of leadership. The Greek word indicates a "divine spark" which manifests itself in eager interest and ardent activity, influencing others to similar concern and zeal. Biographies of great leaders almost always disclose this quality of contagious enthusiasm.

Is its source some mysterious inborn trait? The capacity for enthusiasm is probably innate, but its development and expression must be cultivated. For the Christian it should arise from his "twice-born" experience—the realization that he is in Christ and that Christ is in him, "the hope of glory." The fire must be kept burning by the realization that he has a great Saviour and that he has been saved to witness and to serve. The fire thus kindled, however, must be continuously fed with the fuel of faithfulness and activity.

The Christian's enthusiasm mounts as he worships and learns and is sustained as he puts his faith into practice. By his words and deeds he can challenge others: "Be imitators of me, as I am of Christ" (1 Cor. 11:1).

Perseverance in the face of discouragement.—The admired leader is one who refuses to give up, even in the face of apparent failure. So sure is he of the ultimate triumph of his cause that he refuses to quit, no matter how great the discouragements and disappointments.

Paul remembered the hardships he had suffered in the past and he foresaw persecution and death ahead. Yet, he could say,

"Forgetting what lies behind and straining forward to what lies ahead, I press on toward the goal for the prize of the upward call of God in Christ Jesus" (Phil. 3:13-14).

The Christian leader is not greatly concerned to be known as a "success." Although frequently he may be disappointed and often may regard himself as failing, he will not lose heart. But such a spirit of perseverance is not an instant attainment.

Disappointments may bring discouragement and the temptation to give up. "What's the use?" the tempter may argue. "You know you are failing, you are not appreciated, why not resign?" There may be a few rare spirits who never have such an experience, but the majority will no doubt frankly confess their sympathy for Elijah who, when Jezebel pursued him, prayed that he might die: "O Lord, take away my life; for I am no better than my fathers" (1 Kings 19:4).

As Elijah learned from the "still, small voice" to dispel his depression by obedience, so must the leader, when tempted to give up, learn from his patient church the virtue of perseverance.

Ability to learn and willingness to share.—Limited ability to learn may arise from two conditions: lack of native capacity or lack of opportunity. All persons do not possess equal power to learn. The range of such capability is quite wide. Students in school are often classified as slow, average, or fast learners. There are mentally retarded persons who can scarcely learn at all.

Tests have been devised that determine more or less accurately native mental capacity. It is obviously unfortunate for all concerned if mentally deficient persons are placed in positions of leadership. Since in church circles scientific tests and measurements are impracticable, it is risky to form snap judgments as to mentality of members. Not infrequently persons considered mentally backward have lacked opportunity to develop their abilities. They are like the gems which "the dark unfathomed caves of ocean bear," or the flower "born to blush unseen, and waste its sweetness on the desert air." Discrimination must be exercised to distinguish between the two types—those deprived by nature of capacity to learn and those whose misfortune it is not to have had educational privilege. The latter, with stimulation and guidance, may become very useful workers in the church.

Of necessity, the leader is in many respects a teacher. To teach is to share oneself—one's knowledge and skills, one's beliefs and ideals, one's experience of religion. What is not possessed cannot be shared, and what is possessed must be shared willingly.

The disqualification of some church members for leadership is poverty of Christian life. Perhaps when they became church members there was little understanding of its meaning. Their Christian experience may never have been warm and vital. They may have lived on the circumference of the Christian life rather than at its center. If this be true, they have too little to share to be effective leaders.

Are they therefore hopeless? Perhaps so, if the church writes them off as useless. Just as the underprivileged child needs more nurture, so the underprivileged church member needs understanding and encouragement to take some part, even though it be minor at the beginning. Sharing comes with enrichment and enrichment makes sharing possible. A church is guilty of neglect if it does not provide opportunity for self-expression and service on the part of its less privileged members, as well as those who have had more advantages.

Good reputation and integrity of character.—Good reputation and integrity of character are demanded of the Christian leader. Reputation is what others think he is; character is what he really is. A good name has to be earned; personal integrity is achieved through daily right choices and conduct.

If perfection of reputation and character were required, who could meet the test? The noblest men and women of the Bible had their faults. Paul confessed himself to be the chief of sinners. He had to outlive his reputation as a murderer and achieve his faithfulness through a long and continuous struggle with the flesh. His victory over sin came not from himself but from Jesus Christ his Lord (see Rom. 7:13-25).

Reputation may or may not be deserved. Sometimes a person with a reputation for honesty will turn out to be a rascal. Likewise, one with a shady reputation may prove to be thoroughly trustworthy. A mistake can be outlived. If the leaders of a church were only those who had never suffered criticism, they would either be such paragons of virtue as to be "out of this world" or they would have never done anything worth noticing! Not reputation but character is the ultimate test.

"Man looks on the outward appearance, but the Lord looks on the heart" (1 Sam. 16:7).

It is of course highly important that Christian leaders have both good reputation and good character, but judgment should not be too quickly and firmly formed. Reputation and character come by way of growth. After all, a church is made up of "sinners saved by grace." The Scripture passage is very explicit: "If a man is overtaken in any trespass, you who are spiritual should restore him in a spirit of gentleness. Look to yourself, lest you too be tempted" (Gal. 6:1).

It will not ordinarily be wise to put a weak member in a position of church responsibility in order to strengthen him. But it would be unchristian to exclude him from all consideration because of alleged or even known weakness. A less conspicuous place of service may lead to a higher level of responsibility.

Moral perfection is the ideal toward which the Christian leader should strive, but he must not refuse to serve until he has attained it.

Effective Christian leadership is consecrated and dedicated discipleship. Before a leader can attract and maintain a following, he must himself have learned how to follow. There must be a sense of call to which there is given an affirmative answer. In the biblical sense, the consecration or devotion of a person to a cause or task is primarily God's part; dedication or self-giving is on man's part. God's call is met by man's response if leadership is to be effectual.

Awareness of God's call may be immediate or gradual. Like Samuel, who did not immediately perceive that God was calling him, the Christian may be led by time and circumstance to realize that God wants to consecrate him for a special cause. Likewise, the response may be at once or by stages. Often there is divine use of human instrumentality in evoking the reply, "Here I am" to the question, "Whom shall I send, and who will go for us?" (Isa. 6:8). God does not compel such a reply from an unhearing and unheeding person. Growing awareness of God's presence and purpose and willingness to respond and obey are essential ingredients of consecration.

A church should never lose faith in the power of a transforming conversion experience or a life-changing rededication to Christ. Christ's hardest case was Saul the Pharisee, who became Paul the apostle. Satan's leader won may become one of the most effective leaders for Christ and the church.

Devotion to the task and loyalty to the cause.—Underlying all other qualities, the leader must have faith in Christ, confidence in his redemptive purpose and power, and loyalty to his church and its fellowship.

Feigned and faltering faith in the cause he represents is fatal to the leader of any undertaking. This false note will somehow, sooner or later, be detected and the insincere would-be leader will be rejected. The sin that Jesus condemned most severely was hypocrisy (Matt. 23:13-31).

Gross hypocrisy, however, is not usually the fault that causes the church leader to fail. Rather, it may be a form of disloyalty that brings creeping paralysis from absorption in the secular, a coldness of heart that results from too close identification with the world.

Jesus warns, "No one can serve two masters. . . . You cannot serve God and mammon" (Matt. 6:24). When love of the world and the things of the world overmasters love of Jesus Christ and his cause, leadership is blocked.

Paul wrote sadly of the loss of Demas the deserter, who was "in love with this present world" (2 Tim. 4:10).

Confessedly in today's culture it is not easy to possess and maintain singleness of loyalty to Christ and the fellowship of his faithful disciples. The pull of the world is strong for most of us. Loyalty may at first be weak and at times may falter.

The early churches faced the problem of what to do with the "lapsed"—those who under pressure of persecution denied Christ. Disloyalty was not condoned, but restoration was sought on the basis of repentance and forgiveness. Paul stated the principle: "As for the man who is weak in faith, welcome him, but not for disputes over opinions. Why do you pass judgment on your brother?" (Rom. 14:1,10).

The case is covered in this exhortation: "Encourage the fainthearted, help the weak, be patient with them all" (1 Thess. 5:14). A church who does this may often discover and develop leaders from unpromising material.

Some Inquiries and Conclusions

Above is a list of qualities to be desired and sought by the leader, especially the church leader. In self-examination, these questions may be asked: (1) In what measure do I already possess these qualities? (2) Of which of these qualities do I most keenly feel the lack? (3) How have I come to possess those qualities which I can claim? (4) How can I acquire those qualities which I lack and desire? (5) Wherein do I need improvement of my strong points? (6) What can I do to eliminate my weaknesses? (7) How can I share with others in this process of improvement and achievement?

Turning from oneself to others who are in positions of church leadership, according to the ten statements of qualifications listed, what appear to be the strong points most often noted? the weak points? What are your conclusions (and that of your group) concerning the level of leadership in your church?

Such an analysis may in some cases bring discouragement. However, encouragement will immediately emerge when possibilities rather than actualities are emphasized. In almost every case, including yourself, it will be noted that, with the Holy Spirit's guidance, individual and group effort, and a consistent program of improvement provided by the church, strong points can be still further strengthened and weaknesses transformed into strength. The leadership base is thus broadened and may include those who might otherwise have been excluded.

May we then conclude that the minimum requirements of Christian leadership are: (1) A genuine conversion experience—repentance of sin and saving faith in the Lord Jesus Christ; (2) interest in and concern for people; (3) ability and willingness to learn; (4) membership in a church that manifests faith, hope, and love and seeks to provide the nurture that a good mother would give her children.

Does this mean lowering the standard of leadership until almost any church member could qualify? We turn to the example of Jesus for the answer. He had before him the choice of leaders from the highly trained and well educated rabbis of the Pharisees or from the relatively untrained and uneducated. He passed by the former group and chose the apostles from the latter. Why?

The rabbis were neither approachable nor teachable. Their minds were closed and they were unwilling to change. The men whom Jesus chose were approachable and teachable. They were willing to give Jesus a hearing and joined his company as learners (disciples). They were strong in some of the points listed above but in some of them they were notably weak. Jesus saw in them possibilities of what they might become. He took them as they were and made them into the leaders they became.

Later, just as Jesus had made leaders of the fishermen, he made a leader of Saul, one of the most brilliant of the rabbis, but not until he had humbly asked, "What shall I do, Lord?" (Acts 22:10). These were all willing to listen, learn, and obey. Jesus can make leaders (servants) of his church today those who will meet the simple conditions.

Toward Solving the Leadership Problem

A procedure is now indicated for improving present church leaders and discovering and enlisting others. The church must lead its people to hear the call of Christ, to be willing to learn, to be ready to serve where they are needed, and to desire to improve. If they can be successfully challenged to meet these basic requirements, their future as worthy leaders is well assured. Thus, the church leadership problem may be solved.

This procedure will exclude some who are not willing to meet the conditions or do not have the capacity to learn or who refuse to learn or who have no concern for improvement. Within the circle of those not thus excluded are many who are now being overlooked or who have never thought of themselves as belonging to the church's leadership (servantship) group. To them Christ calls, as he did to the fishermen of long ago, "Follow me, and I will make you become" (Mark 1:17).

Divine and human factors work together. The call to leadership is a call to prepare. In the divine economy, God uses human instrumentality to accomplish his purposes. The human means may be weak and sometimes even unworthy; but, speaking humanly, God has to begin with man where he is. It is encouraging to read that he "chose what is weak in the world to shame the strong" (1 Cor. 1:27), and to learn that God's heroes of faith "won strength out of weakness" (Heb. 11:34). One who feels keenly his deficiency but is assured that God has called him to the task can say with Paul, "I thank him who has given me strength for this, Christ Jesus our Lord, because he judged me faithful by appointing me to his service" (1 Tim. 1:12).

God's call carries with it the sure promise of enablement if the conditions of the call are met. Whether one is praised or even noticed makes little difference if he who called to the task is pleased. Christopher Morley wrote:

> Out for my evening stroll
> I discovered on 84th Street
> A power-house, quietly humming to itself,
> And though I lived nearby
> I had never known it was there.
> Some people are like that.

Something to Think and Pray About

On a scale of zero to ten, how would you rate yourself with respect to each of the ten desirable qualifications listed? What is your estimated average for the total list?

What appear to be your strong points? your weak points? Will your weaknesses bar you from leadership? What can you do about them?

Select a representative group of leaders in your church and rate their strong and weak points as above. On the whole, are they estimated to be below average, above average, about average? What do you conclude?

If God calls, will he also enable? What are the divine and what are the human elements in the call to leadership?

Whom are you trying to please?

4 Progress Through Planned Preparation

An essential of leadership and leadership education is planning for progress. Planning is the link—too often the missing link—between purpose and performance.

Progress requires planning. The wise traveler makes his chart before he starts. The wise builder demands a blueprint before he begins building. "Never cross a bridge until you get to it" is really not a wise adage. Better be sure there is a bridge if a stream is to be crossed! Planning requires looking ahead, foreseeing difficulties and opportunities, determining ahead of time what will be necessary for reaching the desired objective.

Progress is a correlative of planning. Progress necessitates a starting point, a foreseen destination, and successive intermediate points on the way. More progress has been made along some lines during the past one hundred years than in all previous history. The "scientific method," which largely accounts for this progress, is in the main a process of inductive planning—going from the particular to the general, according to planned tests and measurements in the search for the desired results. Back of all planning and research is the infinitely wise God who created the universe, including man, according to a divine plan.

Everyone who bears leadership responsibility or who looks forward to such leadership should be, and must be, a planner.

Other things being equal, the most fruitful leader will be one who has made a plan and followed it.

Planned Preparation Brings Rich Rewards

Planning preparation for leadership is not only necessary but also highly rewarding.

Planned preparation gives poise. The price of unprepared performance is nervousness, uneasiness, often embarrassment and "stage fright." The strain of this condition is more exhausting than the activity itself. The well prepared leader is at ease, because he has thought through what he will say and do and with practice gains the poise essential to effectiveness.

Planned preparation inspires confidence. The well prepared leader is, first of all, confident of himself. He has the assurance of knowing where he is going. He has a road map he can trust. The leader thus assured of himself begets confidence in his followers. They may not always agree with him and he may change direction as he shares his views with his followers, but he steadfastly moves toward a desired goal, because, through previous study, he knows it to be right. Self-confidence and the confidence of others arise from tested preparation.

Planned preparation provides needed resources. The leader must be prepared to meet unexpected emergencies. Leadership would be easy if everything went according to plan.

What shall be done when unexpected difficulty comes? At this juncture the leader must be able to summon help from his background of experience and study. He will recall something that he has read or that a teacher has said that throws light on the problem. Without such background of preparation, the leader may try to ignore the obstacle or blindly collide with it or give up in despair. With adequate resources to draw on, he will remove the obstacle or work around it or make a detour.

Planned preparation involves continuous study. Life is not static. Conditions change, new opportunities and difficulties appear. What once worked well may no longer suffice. Methods that were adequate a generation ago may be totally inadequate today and today's ways may not meet the demands of tomorrow. The textbooks that were once studied need to be supplemented or even replaced by newer ones.

The story is told of a college professor who was called in for a conference with the dean. The dean was troubled, for students were refusing to enrol for the professor's electives and took his required course under protest. The teacher sadly admitted that this was true. "I just don't understand it," he said. "When I came twenty years ago, my classes were crowded with students eager to listen to my lectures. I don't understand it," he repeated. "They are the same lectures." He had too long ago finished his preparation and now he was finished.

There is no such thing as *completing* an education. The teacher is discounted by his students when they realize that he is not keeping up with contemporary thought. "Graduation" means regular progression; "commencement" indicates readiness to begin.

The leader must never cease to learn. Fresh preparation must be made for every performance. Regardless of how many times a musician has played a piece, he must continuously practice. The actor must never cease rehearsing. The preacher knows that something is lost from the sermon if he repeats it without fresh study. The speaker grows dull who goes before his audience with materials that have not been reviewed and renewed. The discipline of such preparation may be severe, but the results will be highly gratifying, both to the leader and to those he leads.

Invite Spiritual Guidance

Let it not be concluded that reading, study, and planning lessen the necessity for spiritual guidance. The Holy Spirit's presence is promised in an emergency where human wisdom is inadequate, but his guidance is equally available in the study, in the quiet moments of reading and reflection, in the processes of preparation. Enduement with the power of the Holy Spirit came to the disciples in the upper room only after they were prepared to receive it. It would indeed grieve the Holy Spirit if he were shut out from the leader's preparation for his duties.

Contrast the hasty, careless preparation sometimes made by church leaders with that made by leaders in other fields. It is said that for a typical television program at least an hour of rehearsal is required for every minute the show is on the screen. Months and even years of preparation often go into the production of a motion picture. Athletes spend long hours in grueling practice for even one game. Musicians spend far more time playing privately than they do in public performance.

To be sure, these are professionals and their success depends on their continuous and arduous preparation. While like time and effort are not to be expected of the volunteer church leader, he should not take lightly the serious task of Christian leadership.

A student in the class of Dr. John A. Broadus, great preacher and teacher of preachers of a past generation, objected to the study of the textbook *Preparation and Delivery of Sermons.* The student quoted the promise of Jesus: "Do not be anxious how you are to speak or what you are to say; for what you are to say will be given to you in that hour" (Matt. 10:19). "I believe," he declared, "that if I open my mouth, God will fill it."

Pointing out that Jesus was speaking of the emergency of trial in persecution, the professor called on the class to open wide their mouths and take a deep breath. "See," he said, "the Lord has filled your mouths—with air!" There is no conflict between divine guidance and human effort. Other things being equal, the best leader will be the one who has made the most careful, prayerful preparation.

Utilize Printed Resources

The church leader today is rich in resources of materials and opportunities for study. In almost every community, adult education courses are offered through the public schools or other agencies. College and seminaries provide extension courses in classes or by correspondence. The denomination provides a rich variety of textbooks in all aspects of church life and work. In the regular programmed meetings of church organizations, practical studies are available for the leader's equipment and enrichment. Lack of resources or ignorance of their existence is no longer an excuse. The weakness of the leader may be that of failure to adopt and follow a planned course of study.

Concentrate on Church Study Course Books

Offered by the Baptist Sunday School Board of the Southern Baptist Convention, this course has grown from one little book in three parts, published in 1902, into a library of uniform, inexpensive texts.

The categories of study include survey courses dealing with the fundamentals of the Christian life: Bible study, the Christian home, the Christian life, church membership, doctrine, evangelism, history, leadership, missions, special studies, stewardship, the Christian in the social order, the denomination, understanding the individual, church administration, Sunday School; Training Union; music ministry; Woman's Missionary Union; and Brotherhood.

If once the embarrassment was that of poverty of such materials, now it is almost the embarrassment of riches! How to begin, what to choose, and how to continue progressively toward a goal become problems of the preparation-minded leader.

A planned program of preparation calls for more than the random reading of selected books or attending an occasional group-study class. A program of progress is needed that will provide a well-rounded course of study, leading, by successive steps, to receiving the highest available awards.

Again, an example may be taken from the plan proposed by the Southern Baptist Sunday School Board. In pursuing the Church Study Course from a selected list of books, the leader or prospective leader may work toward the Christian Training Diploma and the Approved Workman Diploma. For each of these there are four levels of progressive achievement.

To receive the Christian Training Diploma, one must satisfactorily complete any five books; for the Red Seal, any five additional book awards; for the Blue Seal, any five further book awards. For the Gold Seal, any five other book awards can be earned, provided the ten required survey books are taken in category 1 and five books from categories 16-18, and/or 19.

For the Approved Workman Diploma, the basic and complete diploma is awarded on satisfactory completion of five books in one of these categories: 16, 17, 18, or 19.

Requirements for the Red Seal are any five additional book awards; the Blue Seal, any five adidtional book awards; and the Gold Seal, any five aditional book awards, provided at least one has been taken from each of the following categories: 2, 5, 8, 9, 13, and 15. (Write to your Baptist state convention for full and more recent information concerning recommended courses of study.)

Consider the Life and Work Curriculum

Along with the study of books is a planned program of leadership advancement through week-by-week participation in training services following the "Life and Work Curriculum." These materials are not a substitute for leadership training textbooks but are supplemental. They have the advantage of weekly continuity, combining study, discussion, and practice. Undated materials make it possible for the studies to begin at any time and to continue as long as desired.

Much attention is given to the development of specific skills: how to lead a discussion; how to study and interpret the Bible, how to use Bible helps; how to pray; how to learn from Jesus; how to depend on and follow the Holy Spirit's guidance; how to be a soul-winning witness; how to counsel those in trouble; how to be a good steward of all of life; how to become a better church member; how to exercise discernment and make decisions; how to teach and make disciples; how to meet the objections of doubters and unbelievers; how to share in the ministry of music; how to be active in the work and support of worldwide missions; how to be a Christian homemaker; and how to be a good citizen. The list will grow as other needs appear.

In this curriculum, attention is not only given to the "how" or methods but also to the "what" or content and the "why" or purpose. The intent of the continued and purposeful use of these materials is "that the man [or woman] of God may be complete, equipped for every good work" (2 Tim. 3:17).

Study Systematically

What do you do when you *study?* This question is not directed to the student in school but rather to one who has leadership responsibility for which he must prepare. Here are some tested suggestions:

Adopt a time schedule and find a quiet place where study can be carried on. A regular time for study is important. A place conducive to study is helpful. When the appointed time has arrived, nothing but an emergency should be permitted to interfere. The place of study should be protected from the blare of radio or television, noisy conversation or activity, unnecessary interruptions. Not always can such conditions be met, but to the extent that they can, study will be facilitated.

Have at hand the tools of study: Bible and printed helps; names of key persons to be dealt with and basic information concerning them; office accessories—pen, paper, typewriter, clips, folders, filing cabinet or deep desk drawers. Tools do not make the workman, but they help him to be a better workman.

Sit for awhile in quiet meditation and prayer. Martin Luther, the leader of the Protestant Reformation, is said to have remarked that he had so much to do he had to spend at least half the day in prayer. In such prayerful meditation, insights often come that are more valuable than conclusions reached by logic. This is especially true if reasoning is accompanied by worry. "In quietness and in trust shall be your strength" (Isa. 30:15).

Take a problem-solving attitude. Preparatory thinking is a problem-solving process. Ask: What is the real difficulty? Often the heart of the matter is concealed by attendant complications— personality conflicts, wounded pride, prejudices, misunderstandings, petty jealousies, traditional loyalties, and the like. Get the essential problem out into the open, define and clarify it.

Explore possible solutions. If one direction is taken, what will be the probable outcome? If an opposite pathway is followed, what may result? What other alternatives are there and what will be likely to happen if in turn each should be chosen?

Select the most favorable solution and then follow through. "Test everything; hold fast what is good" (1 Thess. 5:21).

Seek experienced counsel. Books are stored-up wisdom. In the Bible is to be found the highest wisdom. Almost always there are living and available persons who have had experience in similar situations. Consultation with a resource person will almost certainly bring needed light.

Utilize the experimental method. The scientist tries out a process under controlled (laboratory) conditions and records the results. He varies the conditions and notes the difference that the variation makes. He weeds out errors and failures and concentrates attention on what works best. This method of experimentation accounts for much of the amazing progress made in developing new processes during the past century. The church leader may apply many of these essentials to the solution of problems that arise.

Put conclusions into practice. The "pure researcher" may not be concerned with the application of his findings, but the practical man will ask, "What's the use?" Both types of investigators are needed. But if no practical use is ever found for the discovery it will usually be shelved as having little consequence. So it is in the world of human need that the church exists. If nothing is done about it, the "talk cure" has little lasting effect.

Communicate effectively the outcome of creative study. Preparation is incomplete, no matter how sound the reasoning, until findings have been reduced to writing or speech so as to be shared with others. "How can I get across to others what I have learned through my study?" is the leader's crucial question. The leader then becomes the teacher, the preacher, the persuader, the promoter, with a sense of mission to communicate to others what study has disclosed to him.

Correlate Church Organizations

Welcome advance was made in leadership training when plans of the several church organizations were correlated. Historically, these organizations had grown up independently. As each organization developed and its functions multiplied, duplications and sometimes unwholesome competitions resulted. After many years of cooperative consultations, representatives of the several church program organizations reached agreement as to how their curriculum materials would be directed toward certain common goals.

Of course, materials vary according to the genius of the respective organizations, but they are now so correlated as to reinforce one another and promote together the major purposes of the church. Sunday School lesson materials, Training Union program materials, Woman's Missionary Union and Brotherhood materials, and Church Music Ministry emphases concentrate on the same themes at the same time.

The church as a whole, in a given quarter, will emphasize and reaffirm its commitment to God: the Sunday School will study the story of redemption; Woman's Missionary Union, response to God; the Brotherhood, God's concern for people; and the Music Ministry will feature a cantata titled *The Dawn of Redeeming Grace;* Training Union will major on how to study the Bible.

Monotony and repetition are avoided, but there is unity in diversity and teamwork in making the church more effective. In all of this, leaders are given practice in sharing and opportunities to learn by doing.

Intensify Spiritual Power

The church leader leads by virtue of what he is even more than what he knows and does. Such leadership requires spiritual power that comes from continuous nurture of the spiritual life. An ounce of the spirit of Christ is worth more than a pound of cold logic. Gifts of the Spirit are more to be cultivated than gifts of skill. Although the leader speaks eloquently and has prophetic powers and understands all mysteries and all knowledge and has faith to remove mountains, if he has not love he is nothing (cf. 1 Cor. 13:1-2).

The spiritual life must be nurtured or it will grow anemic and powerless. The means of this nurture is obvious: daily Bible study and prayer; regularly attending and participating in services of worship; habitual practice of Christian stewardship; self-forgetting service of others.

Jesus stated the conditions in terms that cannot be ignored: "I am the vine, you are the branches. He who abides in me, and I in him, he it is that bears much fruit, for apart from me you can do nothing. . . . If you abide in me, and my words abide in you, ask whatever you will, and it shall be done for you. By this my Father is glorified, that you bear much fruit, and so prove to be my disciples" (John 15:5-8). If the branch cannot bear fruit apart from the vine, so the Christian cannot be fruitful unless there is unbroken union with Christ.

Leadership is not a special gift with which a few exceptional persons are endowed. It is a right to be earned, an ability to be learned, a privilege to be won. Requirements must be met; disciplines undergone; hours of study spent; sacrifices made; earnest prayer engaged in; self-will surrendered to God's will; and love and service of self replaced by love and service of others for Christ's sake—guidance from self-interest replaced by guidance of the Holy Spirit.

Jesus never promised that the way would be easy; rather, he declared that it would be the way of the cross, even of suffering and of death. Plainly he said, "If any man would come after me, let him deny himself and take up his cross and follow me" (Matt. 16:24).

The unplanned life will come to its close in disappointment.

God has a plan for every life, but he has given each one the right to accept or reject or neglect his plan. Each stage of life should be preparation for the next, until the curtain goes down when time becomes eternity. Every activity of preparation for Christian leadership is also preparation for living the abundant life which Jesus said he came to give.

There are many investments of life which can be made, some of which may be promising but will end in loss. There is one investment which will never fail and will continue to bear dividends forever—investment in the lives of others for Christ's sake.

The leader who thus discovers and fits into the divine plan for his life and charts a course accordingly need not adopt a fatalistic attitude that leaves out effort on his part. God's election for salvation and service carries with it responsibility for choice and endeavor.

Men are not robots, controlled by taped instructions; they are free agents and can say yes or no to God. They can use their talents to gain more. Or, they can neglect to use what God has entrusted them with and lose what they have. Paul points to the tragic possibility of frustrating or nullifying the grace of God (Gal. 2:21). God furnishes the plan, but the Christian leader must make it operational through planned progress. John Oxenham asks:

> Is your place a small place?
> Tend it with care!
> He set you there.
>
> Is your place a large place?
> Guard it with care!
> He set you there.
>
> Whate'er your place, it is
> Not yours alone, but His
> Who set you there.

Something to Think and Pray About

What is the relation between progress and planning?

Why is planned preparation necessary for leadership? What are consequences of failure to plan and prepare?

How adequately do you and your fellow church workers plan for leadership duties? How does this compare with specialists in other fields of public service?

How well acquainted are you with available resources of preparation for and improvement of your leadership? Does your church sponsor a planned program of study courses?

How well correlated are the several church organizations? Do they cooperate effectively in leadership training plans?

Will emphasis on planned preparation tend to despiritualization? Why?

What influence will faithful planning and performance of church leadership duties have on enrichment of the whole of life?

5 The Job, the Objectives, the Methods

You are holding or preparing for a place of responsibility in the church that involves leadership. Some questions arise: Just what is the job, generally and specifically? What are the objectives in performance of your duties? What methods will be employed?

Begin with the job description. Suppose the position is that of pastor or staff member, or deacon or church officer, Sunday School officer or teacher, Training Union officer or leader, officer or leader in the men and women's organizations, responsibility for Music Ministry, or committee chairmanship. Abstractly, what is the principal *leadership* function of the position? Concretely, what are the particulars?

The pastor as leader is described in the New Testament by the word *episcopos*. This word is translated in the Authorized Version as "bishop" and is defined in the Greek lexicon as "overseer"—one charged with the duty of seeing that things to be done by others are done right. Employed staff members have more specific responsibilities than the pastor. Deacons are "servants of the church," responsible with pastor and staff to promote and conserve the church's welfare. The church treasurer will not only receive and account for finances but will also lead in developing the church in Christian stewardship. The church clerk will keep accurate records but will also lead in keeping the church informed about itself and the perpetuation of its history.

Heads of the several church organizations and their associates will not only perform their administrative duties efficiently but will also lead in maintaining the highest possible level of organizational efficiency and spiritual fruitfulness. The teachers and workers with classes and groups will not only instruct and conduct meetings but will also lead their members to put into practice what they have learned.

Beyond leadership in the church will be leadership in other areas—the community, school, business and society, the state, nation, and world—as opportunities may afford.

Objectives Determined

Having answered generally and specifically the question, "What is my job?" the inquiry then becomes, "What are my objectives?" Authoritative writers on the subject place high in the list of leadership responsibilities the clear statement of aims. Aimless leadership is bound to be weak and unattractive. More leadership failure is probably due to indirection than to lack of ability.

John Dewey, in his *Democracy and Education*, concludes that "a man is stupid or blind or unintelligent . . . just in the degree in which in any activity he does not know what he is about; namely, the probable consequences of his acts."

Why are clearly defined objectives necessary?

An objective determines the direction in which the leader proposes to go. Decision concerning this direction will not be arbitrarily made by the leader but will be determined in consultation with others. Lacking such direction, both leader and followers will arrive at their destination by accident, if at all.

Objectives are necessary because they save time and energy. If the goal is not clearly perceived from the beginning, wasteful detours and bypaths will be taken that slow down and endanger the undertaking. Many good causes have been abandoned because followers of an aimless leader grew tired of activities that seemed to get nowhere.

Objectives are necessary because they determine the means required for their achievement. "Count the cost!" Jesus admonished. The cost may be in terms of money or materials or labor or time; whatever the cost, it should be foreseen in relation to the end in view. Too late, it may be discovered that the necessary means is not available or that the leader's followers are not willing to pay the price.

Objectives are necessary in order to maintain morale. When there is no foreseen goal, discouraged followers are tempted to quit. Leader and followers lose heart if they do not understand the purpose of what they are doing.

Objectives are necessary in order to measure progress. "How are we doing?" can best be answered in terms of progress toward a goal. Rarely is the goal reached without intermediate steps. Progress may sometimes seem painfully slow. But if it is understood that each stage brings the undertaking that much nearer to consummation, willingness to keep going is maintained.

Objectives are necessary in order to motivate intelligent prayer and the seeking of spiritual guidance. James states the case when he writes, "You do not have, because you do not ask. You ask and do not receive, because you ask wrongly" (James 4:2-3).

Prayer that has no clear purpose and does not seek the Holy Spirit's guidance toward a worthy goal will not be pleasing to God, nor will it bring the needed blessing. The God of supreme intelligence and will desires that those who serve him do so intelligently and purposefully. He will guide in determining objectives and he will also help those who cooperate with him sensibly in achieving foreseen ends.

Aims Evaluated

What are some marks of good aims?

A good aim possesses relevance; that is, it is related to an actual situation of need and opportunity. What may once have been a worthy objective may no longer be so in changed circumstances. An objective suitable for one type of church and community may be unsuited to another. In setting up an objective, a good question is: To what extent is it calculated to get the results that we desire?

A good objective will be subject to change as conditions change. The difficulty with trying to follow a standardized statement of aims is that it may not permit sufficient freedom and flexibility. The "standard" is intended to be an instrument of measurement, not a hard-and-fast statement of unbending rules. It is more important, for example, for a Sunday School to reach people than to reach the Standard! The two objectives are not mutually exclusive but the printed guide should not be made an end in itself.

The mark of a sound objective is that it is not a fixed goal but moves forward as it is approached. If a given objective is reached and there is nothing beyond, stagnation ensues. When the leader and group can say with self-satisfaction, "Now we have it made!" they will probably begin a downgrade movement—they may stand still, but the situation moves ahead.

A good objective will challenge to creativeness—to new solutions to meet new problems as they arise. There is danger that in trying to reach a stated objective, freedom will be restrained. The objective should always include more than just the end being sought; it should take into account the development of individual initiative and creative group thinking. The result will be too dearly bought if the price is the loss of liberty and originality.

A good objectve will be more concerned with what happens to persons than what is achieved materially. Edwin Markham reminds us that "nothing is worth the making if it does not make the man." While this essentially is true in any undertaking, it is especially true in a Christian enterprise. Some of the gravest mistakes in church leadership have been made at this point—lack of concern for the personal equation.

In all that Jesus Christ said and did we see this truth shining forth—his measure of value in terms of persons. We hear him indignantly exclaim, when he was criticized for healing a man on the sabbath, "Of how much more value is a man than a sheep!" (Matt. 12:12). Obeying the rule in order to achieve the objective must always be subordinated to human welfare.

The question to which the principles above have been leading now becomes: What are the distinctive objectives of Christian leadership? It is clear that defining such objectives, in the nature of the case, cannot be a one-man affair. The leader is a servant of servants, a laborer together with God and others. Ordway Tead states that leadership "is the activity of influencing people to cooperate toward some goal which they come to find desirable." Accordingly the leader will not say, "This is what I think should be done—let's do it!" but rather, "This is what we agree needs to be done—let me help you!" An essential function will be to lead the group to agreement as to what the objective is.

The most obvious objective is to get the job done. The characteristic American spirit is expressed in Abbie Farwell Brown's poem "Work":

> Work! that makes the red blood glow,
> Work, that makes the quick brain glow.
> Plough and hammer, hoe and flails
> Axe and crowbar, saw and nails . . . .
> Thank God for work!

And a favorite American church song is "To the Work." There is of course virtue in worthy activity, but the objective needs to be broader than getting the job done.

Antecedent conditions must be considered before an ultimate objective can be achieved. What difficulties must be overcome? In battle, the general knows that objective A must be taken before objective B can be reached and the final objective C achieved. Rarely is anything of value accomplished without first removing obstacles in the way. The leader must take a good, hard look at hindrances and make their removal a prior objective. Faith in ultimate success under divine guidance does not obviate the necessity of foresight and the use of human means to provide ways of dealing with impediments to progress.

An important secondary objective is the procurement of necessary supplies for the undertaking. The military term is *logistics*, the scientific study of material requirements—provisions, arms, ammunition, for the armed forces if they are to wage war successfully. In a church project the objective may be ever so spiritual but there will almost certainly be need of money, facilities, resources of communication, varied instrumentalities in order to press the project to its completion. To assume that God alone will provide these practical necessities is not faith but presumption. He has given men minds with which to think and to plan and he expects them to do their part. An essential objective of good leadership is not only foresight of ends but the obtaining of necessary means.

The distinctive mark of the Christian objective is its person-mindedness. The Bible is a person-minded book, its revelations coming through and gathering about persons. The triune God is supremely personal—Father, Son, Holy Spirit. The biblical writers concentrate attention on persons, about whom and for whom they wrote. Concern for persons characterizes every book of the Bible. Of the founders of the world's great religions, Jesus Christ is supremely the most person-minded.

Whatever the activity, the leader's determinative question should be, What will this do for and to persons? Organizational and administrative objectives, money-raising, building and equipment, enlargement campaigns, educational improvement, enrichment of worship, increased effectiveness of proclamation and evangelism, outreach through visitation and mission, plans for social action—none of these is properly a Christian objective apart from persons. The leader should be more concerned for the outcomes in winning persons to Christ and in developing Christian character than in the tangible success of a specific undertaking.

Beyond and above all other objectives is the will of God. The leader's guiding question is not so much what we want but what God wills. To discover and obey God's will is seldom easy. Self-will must be gotten out of the way, the purposes of Jesus Christ must be studied and understood, the guidance of the Holy Spirit must be accepted.

There must be willingness to follow divine direction. Time spent in determining this objective is never wasted but will prove far more valuable than planning that leaves God out.

Jesus said, "If any man's will is to do his [God's] will, he shall know" (John 7:17). Again he said, "I am the light . . .; he who follows me will not walk in darkness" (John 8:1). Supremely, the Christian leader's objective is to find the will of God and to follow the leadership of Jesus Christ.

From analysis of the job and its objectives, the leader will turn to methods of leading. Method will depend on a number of circumstances: the personality of the leader, characteristics of the group to be led, the nature and purposes of the undertaking, and resources and limitations. The leader will do well to examine critically the several possibilities of exercising leadership.

Mistaken Ways of Leading

Command.—The leader may conceive of himself as the commanding officer of a company of soldiers. Tennyson epitomizes the unquestioned obedience to military authority in his "Charge of the Light Brigade." Notwithstanding that "someone had blundered" in giving the order, he writes:

> Theirs not to make reply,
> Theirs not to reason why,
> Theirs but to do and die.
> Into the valley of Death
> Rode the six hundred:

Such blind obedience to an authoritarian leader is completely contrary to the Christian view of leadership. History records the rise and power of leaders like this, but it also records their downfall. When the dictator type leader arises, in church or state, the truism of Lord Acton, the nineteenth-century political philosopher, needs to be remembered: "Power tends to corrupt; absolute power corrupts absolutely."

Manipulation.—The leader who seeks to lead by manipulation uses the method of the "wire-puller"—one who stands in the background and gets what he wants by using others. Such a leader "plays a part." The New Testament describes him as a "hypocrite." He is the familiar political character who poses as a servant of the people while actually feathering his own nest. He tries to get by flattery what he knows he could not get by direct command. He is concerned for results but always with an eye to his own self-interest.

For a time the manipulator may seem to succeed. But eventually his true character will appear and he is repudiated by the people. This is more certain to be true in the church circle than in the secular, for Christianity abhors double-dealing.

Suggestion.—To suggest is often more effective than to command or to manipulate. Advertisers realize the power of suggestion. They seek to lead customers to buy their products by associating them with catchy music, attractive pictures, health and happiness, security and prosperity. Parents know that it is often easier to get their children to obey by suggestion than by compulsion.

Psychologists make much of suggestion in obtaining desired response. This is a legitimate method of leadership if it is practiced sincerely and worthily. Suggested alternatives open the way to discussion that may well lead to conclusions that the group adopts as its own. Yet, the one who suggests must avoid the deadly trap of using the method for ulterior ends.

Better Ways of Leading

Instruction.—Presumably the leader who gives instructions occupies his leadership position because he is better acquainted with the task than others. At least he knows where to get the information. He may therefore instruct the group as to procedure, positively and negatively, in order to get desired results. He may drill on the printed materials until they are fixed in memory. He may repeat customary practices until they become established habits. He may ask questions and correct mistaken answers until there is uniformity.

The method of drill and recitation will be valuable as long as the leader does not arbitrarily demand verbatim responses. Stereotyped instruction may entrench the status quo, thereby impeding progress. In a world of change, sound instruction will take account of new conditions and new ways. It will keep in line with developing problems and processes; else, it will invite stagnation.

Persuasion.—To persuade is to convince. By argument or entreaty it changes minds and the direction of activity. Persuasion may be through direct or indirect appeal. The persuasive leader may seek to change belief or behavior by presentation of facts, by logical reasoning, or by stirring the emotions. Indeed, all of these elements may be present in persuasion.

Persuasion may be less direct—through example, through word association, through illustration, through prejudice and appeal to self-interests, through the attraction of noble ideals, through excitement to fear or incitement to courage, and through dread of punishment or hope of reward.

Preaching at its best is a notable and effective example of direct persuasion. Biography, poetry, fiction, history, and dramatics are less direct but often powerful means of persuasion. Paul writes concerning himself and his fellow Christians, "Therefore, knowing the fear of the Lord, we persuade men" (2 Cor. 5:11).

Leadership is at its best when persuasion is used to convince men to believe the claims of Christ and to follow his way of life. However, persuasion may be misused if it is employed for selfish purposes, or to stir up prejudices, or to arouse unworthy emotions, or to alienate men from God and one another.

Persuasion is a powerful means both for good and evil. To be Christian, it must be under obedience to Christ and the guidance of the Holy Spirit.

Sharing.—This is the most satisfying way of leading.

There may be times when imperative command and unhesitating obedience are necessary, as in an emergency when life or a sacred principle is at stake. When tempers and prejudices get out of hand, circumstances may justify the leader's employing diplomatic indirection and suggestion. Persuasion is often the recourse when appeal to reason and feeling is needed to induce right attitude and action or to change wrong direction of thinking and believing. Almost always the good leader is a teacher, instructing his followers as one charged with their guidance.

The principle that saves any of these methods from going astray is that of Christian sharing—love in action. Jesus put this first, "This is my commandment, that you love one another as I have loved you" (John 15:12).

Paul restates the principle: "He who loves his neighbor has fulfilled the law. The commandments . . . are summed up in this sentence, 'You shall love your neighbor as yourself.' . . . therefore love is the fulfilling of the law" (Rom. 13:8-10).

Activated by this principle, the Christian leader, no matter how high and responsible his position, will think of himself simply as "first among equals." He will therefore share himself, his knowledge and ability, his devotion to Christ and the church, his sense of call and his enthusiasm for the task, his compassion for the lost and his respect for the saved, his willingness to serve and to sacrifice. He will share to the measure of his capacity and thus fulfil his ministry of leadership. Lowell wrote:

> Life is a leaf of paper white
> Whereon each one of us may write
> His word or two, and then comes night.
>
> Greatly begin! though thou have time
> But for a line, be that sublime,—
> Not failure, but low aim, is crime.

Something to Think and Pray About

Stated broadly and in specific detail, what is my leadership job (1) in the church? (2) elsewhere?

How well am I fulfilling my leadership responsibilities?

Why are clearly defined objectives necessary? How fully do I recognize this necessity?

What are the marks of a good aim? How well do my aims meet this test?

What is the distinctive Christian mark of the leader's objectives?

How can I distinguish between immediate, intermediate, and ultimate objectives? On which of these do I place major emphasis?

Beyond human consideration, what is the supreme determinant of the Christian leader's objectives? How well do I meet this test?

What are some wrong ways and what are some right ways of leading? How can I tell the difference?

When is leadership at its best?

6 Achievement Through Teamwork

When, back in the twenties, little Center College's "Praying Colonels" football team defeated mighty Harvard, Captain "Bo" Macmillan was asked how they did it. He replied, "There were eleven men in every play that Center made!"

This is a classic description of teamwork. Kipling, in one of his *Barrack Room Ballads,* made the seasoned old soldier say, "It's not the individual nor the army as a whole, but the ever-lastin' teamwork of every bloomin' soul."

It is recognized in military circles that teamwork is a prime essential of victory. A thrilling example is the D-Day Allied invasion which climaxed World War II. All the armed forces—reconnaissance, air, land, sea—moved as a unit with timed precision that made this daring military maneuver a success. Other things being equal, a church will achieve its highest purposes when its leaders cooperate thus toward common ends.

An Old Testament example of teamwork is the rebuilding of the ruined wall around Jerusalem under the leadership of Nehemiah. "Half of my servants," Nehemiah recorded, "worked on construction, and half held the spears, shields, bows, and coats of mail; and the leaders stood behind all the house of Judah, who were building on the wall" (Neh. 4:16-17).

The wall was long and the workmen were necessarily separated from one another. In the event of an attack, Nehemiah instructed: "In the place where you hear the sound of the trumpet, rally to us there. Our God will fight for us" (v. 20).

"So we built the wall," Nehemiah happily concluded.

A New Testament Principle

Jesus Christ took a little company of apparently insignificant men and women, linked them together in an unbreakable unity, and sent them out to win a world.

At the high moment of his redemptive ministry, just before he went to the cross, he interceded for them with the Father, praying: "The glory which thou hast given me I have given to them, that they may be one even as we are one, I in them and thou in me, that they may become perfectly one, so that the world may know that thou hast sent me and hast loved them even as thou hast loved me" (John 17:22-23).

Paul, pleading for unity in the disturbed Corinthian church, declares, "For we are fellow workmen for God" (1 Cor. 3:9). Then he states the principle inclusively: "None of us lives to himself, and none of us dies to himself" (Rom. 14:7).

When Jesus said, "I will build my church," he was evidently thinking of a fellowship of believing disciples. He gave no explicit directions concerning church polity or practice or organization. In the only other recorded statement in which Jesus used the word "church" he gave direction as to how a broken fellowship is to be restored (Matt. 18:15-20). He made it clear that enmity or unforgiveness among his disciples is a cardinal sin (Matt. 6:14-15).

The New Testament Greek word translated "fellowship" is *koinōnia*, meaning literally shared interest or conjoint participation, as when the Jerusalem believers "were together and had all things in common" (Acts 2:44). A church without the spirit of community has violated its charter. Church leaders are under divine obligation to exhibit and maintain team spirit.

To "join the church" is to become a member of the body of Christ. What your body is to you as the instrument of your mind and will, a true church is to Jesus Christ. He has on earth no hands with which to work but those of his disciples, no feet to walk except those that walk for him, no lips to speak except those that bear him witness. Every Christian is therefore commissioned to work, to walk, to speak for him.

Reinforcement of Individuality

There are "varieties of gifts, . . . varieties of service, . . . varieties of working" (1 Cor. 12:4-6). Equality of all believers does not mean a dead level of ability and responsibility. Using the analogy of the human body, Paul points out that in the church there are those who are weaker and stronger, those invested with greater or less honor. Just as in the human body each part is essential to the healthy functioning of the whole, so in the church all members are necessary. "If one member suffers, all suffer together; if one member is honored, all rejoice together" (1 Cor. 12:26).

The leader in the church is of no greater worth as a person than the humblest member; yet he may well be of more service because of the position to which he has been called. His service is enhanced in proportion to his concern "that there may be no discord in the body, but that the members may have the same care for one another" (1 Cor. 12:25).

You are a soul with a body. So long as life lasts on the earth, the two are inseparable. Personality is more and other than a physical being; yet, the spiritual expresses itself through the physical. The human body is the highly organized instrumentality of personality.

The church, likewise, is spiritual in its essential being; yet, it needs togetherness in order to function in a material world. Jesus recognized this necessity for cooperation when he gathered about him a group of baptized believers, formed them into a body of disciples whom he taught and trained, and sent them out, two and two, with detailed instructions as to how they were to bear his message and do his work. After his death and resurrection, he brought together 120 convinced and trusted believers who constituted his church and who began to move out in ever-enlarging circles to fulfil his commission to make disciples, to baptize them, and to teach them (Matt. 28:19-20).

The story of what Jesus "began to do and to teach" continues through the book of Acts and the Epistles. Here, under the Holy Spirit's guidance, the outreach is enlarged. The pattern of organization is changed to meet changing conditions, but basic principles and purposes remain.

Togetherness in Worship and Proclamation

Togetherness is a vital necessity in carrying out the church's purposes. Whatever else a church may or may not do, its members must come together for worship and the proclamation of the redemptive message. Effectiveness requires working together to provide a place, leaders, schedules, outreach, financial support. Lacking these elements, worship and proclamation would be without substance and power.

By its very nature, a Christian church must be a teaching church. An institution for teaching requires organization—officers and teachers, curriculum, orderly procedures, enlistment of students, expressional activities, aims and outcomes, financial support. Such an organization demands togetherness, without which it would soon be in confusion and ultimately would go out of existence.

It is not enough to worship, to proclaim, to teach. A church must train. This requires experience under guidance. Skills are acquired by putting knowledge into practice. A program of training in and for churchmanship, including every member, requires organization—leaders, assistants, sponsors, materials, age groupings, scheduled activities, continuous promotion, guidance materials, church direction and support.

Without organized teamwork, membership-leadership training would have little chance of success.

With the possible exception of Music Ministries, the present complex of organizations in a typical Southern Baptist church originated apart from the churches. One by one they were adopted by the churches and each developed independently of the others, sometimes even in competition.

The Sunday School had its beginning with the "ragged school" of Robert Raikes, a printer and newspaper publisher of Gloucester, England, in 1781. Disturbed by the destitute condition of factory children, Raikes rented a building and hired four women to teach underprivileged children on Sunday. The movement spread and became church-related when church houses and volunteer church members took the place of rented buildings and paid teachers.

The movement came to America and spread rapidly, although not without opposition from the clergy. Baptists of America, with their lay genius and devotion to the Bible, found the Sunday School peculiarly suited to their purpose. Often there was a Sunday School before there was a church and many churches grew out of Sunday Schools. Gradually the Sunday School was incorporated into the life of the churches, although for a long time it was an independent organization, electing its own officers and teachers and paying its own expenses.

Until the latter part of the nineteenth century, women had

little part in affairs of the church. Ladies Aid Societies gave
them some opportunity for service and giving through "bazaars"
and "sales" and personal work. Pastors and lay leaders took
very seriously and exclusively Paul's injunction that the women
should "keep silence" in the church. Women responded much
more readily to the appeal of missions than did their anti-
missionary and "omissionary" pastors and menfolk, so that the
Ladies Aid became—and its successor has remained—primarily
missionary in character.

In 1888, Woman's Missionary Union was organized, much to
the displeasure of many of the brethren. It was designated
"Auxiliary to the Southern Baptist Convention," mainly because
women had no place in the Convention, even as messengers.
In the course of years this attitude has changed, so that now
the official manual is titled *The Woman's Missionary Union
Program of a Church.* Much progress has been made toward full
integration of the organization as a team member of the churches
and the denomination.

Training Union has had a somewhat similar history of beginning outside the churches. Traditionally, young people were
looked upon as young adults and no special provision was made
for them in the work of the churches. Recognition of their
special place and needs led to the organization in 1881 of Young
People's Society for Christian Endeavor, an interdenominational
organization that soon became nationally popular. Dissatisfied
with its doctrinal weakness, Baptists withdrew and organized
Baptist Young People's Union in 1891.

Southern Baptist churches found this movement to their liking
and eventually it was adopted by the Convention. It was
intended at first for young people only, but in 1934 the name
was changed to Baptist Training Union and the age grading
of the Sunday School was adopted. During this process of

change, Training Union has gone from almost complete independence of church and denomination to full recognition as a member of the church and denominational team.

Men of the churches were relatively late and somewhat reluctant in forming a separate organization. In 1906, sporadic organized groups of men of various denominations were united as the Laymen's Missionary Movement, primarily for the purpose of promoting and supporting foreign missions.

Under guidance of able leadership, laymen of the United States and Canada visited mission fields, attended missionary meetings, and responded to the challenge of young mission volunteers to "match their lives with their dollars." Many influential Baptist men engaged in the movement. Recognizing its significance, the Southern Convention affirmed its endorsement and appointed a committee to give it denominational character and direction. In 1916, a secretary was appointed and headquarters established at Knoxville, Tennessee. Sixteen years later the name was changed to Baptist Brotherhood of the South, with headquarters at Memphis. Later, three age divisions were included—Baptist Men, Young Men, and Boys. Again the process is observed—the adoption and denominationalizing of an organization that had its origin outside the churches.

The most recent addition to the accumulated church organizations described above is the Church Music Ministry. Music has always been an inseparable part of church activities. The religion of the Old Testament was a singing religion, and the New Testament makes much of music and song.

In the early years of Baptist church life, music was largely informal and spontaneous. When the "church choir" developed, some semblance of organization was found necessary. As the importance of "music for all" became more fully recognized, the Sunday School Board appointed B. B. McKinney editor of its music publications. In 1937, the Southern Baptist Convention appointed a committee to study the need of a church music program. Statewide music programs began to develop. In 1941, the Sunday School Board added to its staff a director of music activities and publications, which became the officially established Church Music Department.

Problems of Relationships

Problems inevitably arose concerning the "adopted children" of the churches. Should the organizations be independent of the church, interdependent within the church, or under church control? What should be the relation of the organizations to one another—entire separation, competition, toleration, cooperation, correlation? Since a church, according to the New Testament, is a unified body and cannot prosper if divided, the evident relation of its parts is that of correlation. How is this end to be achieved?

The answer lies in the attitudes and intentions of church and denominational leaders. On the local church level, solutions are found in the church council, made up of representatives of the several church organizations and of the church as a whole. Meeting as a cooperative "council for counsel," they seek to obey the divine injunction, "Do nothing from selfishness or conceit, but in humility count others better than yourselves. Let each of you look not only to his own interests, but also to the interests of others" (Phil. 2:3-4).

On the denominational level, solutions are likewise found in the corresponding Inter-Agency Council, bringing together responsible leaders of the Convention boards and agencies for conference and agreement.

The conclusion is clear: leadership without teamwork brings frustration in the complex organization of church and denomination. This truth needs to be recognized and emphasized by everyone in the church charged with any responsibility. With this spirit, a church will move forward, over all difficulties.

The Question of Personal Attitudes

What attitude shall you as a leader take toward these several organizations?

You may assume that your organization is the most important in the church; therefore, it should be given priority. This view may be quite sincere; nevertheless it will almost certainly result in friction. You may look on the several organizations as competitors, each seeking to outdistance the other. While competition may be the "life of trade," it may also prove the death of fellowship. Hurtful church divisions may often be traced to unseemly rivalries among its organizations.

You may ignore the other organizations in concentration of concern for your own. If this spirit prevails, each organization will go its own separate way, with the inevitable weakness that comes from disunity. You may realize the interdependence of the several organizations but have no way to implement this interdependence. The spirit of the church may be improved, but actual cooperation may be lacking.

The remedy for any of these types of fragmentation of the church is in the conscious cultivation of team spirit with practical means of putting it into operation. Under the guidance of pastor, staff members, deacons, and church officers, leaders of the several organizations will see themselves as members of a team, parts of a whole—the church itself.

Thus the church is seen as functioning through its organizations as it worships and proclaims, teaches and trains, enlists and utilizes its total membership, extending its outreach from its Jerusalem to the "uttermost part."

Prerequisites and Values

The development of team spirit must not be left to chance. There are conditions prerequisite to its inception and growth.

Team spirit is based on confidence—on the part of leaders in themselves; on the part of followers in the leaders; and in one another. When confidence is lost, all is lost.

Leaders may make mistakes, followers may blunder. But if they are sincere in it all, their weaknesses can be forgiven and a new beginning made. Confidence is the first essential to be sought, the last to be risked. When leaders and followers genuinely believe in one another, their unity may occasionally be disturbed but not broken.

Team spirit, to be enduring, must be in the interest of a worthy cause. A noted football coach said, concerning the failure of his team to win, "We are not going to have a winning team as long as the players seem to think that winning or losing makes little difference."

The greatest of all causes is the Christian mission. Whatever the undertaking in the church, it should be vitally related to the success of this mission. The particular task in itself may seem small or inconsequential, but if it is seen in the perspective of winnng the lost, building a strong church for a hard world, and carrying out the commission of Christ, it becomes sufficient to motivate the highest form of team spirit.

Team spirit calls for and calls out the best of human capability. It is hard to grow enthusiastic over mediocrity, settling for less than the best of which leaders and followers are capable. In most men and women there are powers which have never been called into play but which will respond when occasion demands. Team spirit runs high when leader and group discover hidden potentialities that are realized in togetherness.

Team spirit springs from and begets creativity. The group

reacts to the challenge of the leader, the leader to the challenge of the group. New ideas and new solutions to problems emerge and team spirit grows as originality develops. Few things are more exciting to the human spirit than to engage in creative actitvity.

Team spirit is maintained by a measure of consummation. There is a tendency to lose interest in an undertaking that seems to get nowhere. There may not always be "success" as the world counts it. But if the task moves forward in accordance with the prayer, "Thy kingdom come, thy will be done," steadfast devotion is maintained in the face of discouragement or even apparent failure.

"Fear not, little flock," Jesus said to the handful of disciples gathered about him, "for it is your Father's good pleasure to give you the kingdom" (Luke 12:32). Later, under fierce persecution, they were sustained by the promise: "The kingdom of the world has become the kingdom of our Lord and of his Christ, and he shall reign for ever and ever" (Rev. 11:15).

A church is undefeatable when, with this team spirit, it is upheld by the certainty of Christ's ultimate kingdom consummation.

Loss and Recovery

Just as team spirit must be nurtured and its skills gained through practice, it may be lost through wrong attitudes and behavior.

Team spirit is inhibited by self-centeredness. The "star performer" may occasionally win a game and get applause, but he will not produce a winning team. The self-centered church worker is a liability, whether he be the pastor or a class secretary. Teamwork gets more done than does individual effort, no matter how brilliant the performer. Paul warns, "If any one thinks he is something, when he is nothing, he deceives himself" (Gal. 6:3); but, it may be added, he deceives no one but himself!

Team spirit is stifled by inconsiderateness. Lack of consideration for the feelings of others is all but fatal to leadership. Wounded pride will usually seek retaliation and thus unity of the group is destroyed.

Team spirit is undermined by unfairness. The leader, in order to make his point or have his way, may resort to stratagems that smack of political trickery. His success will mean the team's failure. Unfairness is remembered long after the end achieved is forgotten. When followers say of the leader, "He took unfair advantage of us," the only unity that survives is that of the rebels who repudiate him. The proverb puts it bluntly: "Lying lips are an abomination to the Lord, but those who act faithfully are his delight" (Prov. 12:22). Paul states the leader's guarantee against disruption of fellowship, "We aim at what is honorable not only in the Lord's sight but also in the sight of men" (2 Cor. 8:21).

Team spirit is weakened by unpreparedness. The leader and those he leads need to bring to the task thought and prayer which assure economy of time and direction of energies. The question answers itself: "If the bugle gives an indistinct sound, who will get ready for battle?" (1 Cor. 14:8).

Team spirit is disrupted by critical-mindedness. Leaders who commend get far better results than those who reprimand. Appreciation kindles much more enthusiasm than disapproval. A simple thank you may be better pay than monetary reward. Team spirit will not thrive in an atmosphere of captious criticism.

Paul almost exhausts language in his appeal to the Philippian Christians for unity and team spirit. He writes: "If there is any encouragement in Christ, any incentive of love, any participation in the Spirit, any affection and sympathy, complete my joy by being of the same mind, having the same love, being in full accord and of one mind. Have this mind among yourselves, which you have in Christ Jesus, who . . . emptied himself, . . . humbled himself and became obedient unto death" (Phil. 2:1-2, 5-8).

Here is the way to gain and maintain that unity in the church for which our Lord prayed the Father, "That they [all] may be one even as we are one, . . . that the world may know" (John 17:22-23). Join Henry B. Robbins in praying:

Grant to us a sense of presence:
Make us all aware of Thee;
May Thy Holy Love unite us
In the bond that sets men free—
Free to understand each other,
Free to claim each as his brother,
Free to build in unity,
Free, O God, but bound to Thee.

Something to Think and Pray About

Measuring your church by this ideal of vital unity, how would you rate it: below average, about average, above average?

Examining yourself, how do you rate?

Do you tend to go it alone, or do you account yourself a good team worker?

Take a frank look at yourself. Do you help or hinder team spirit?

Do you consider working with others more effective and fruitful than working alone?

Do you pray for that unity of faith and action that will build up the body of Christ (his church) at home and overseas?

7 Changed Ways for Changing Times

Education, once thought of as confined to a schoolhouse, is carried on today in a variety of ways and situations. Perhaps the most significant modern development in education is the changed view as to how and where and for whom education is provided.

The church must recover its right to be called an educational institution, and the growing edge will be the selection and education of its leaders. The church has a distinctive field of opportunity in the continued education of young people and adults. It will not undertake general education but will do well to stick to its specialty—religion. Here it has almost a monopoly. But if it measures up to its responsibility, the church must concentrate on its leaders and provide for them a variety of methods of learning to lead.

Today's churches are more fortunate than their predecessors in the provisions available for leadership education. In today's world, with its rapid and radical change, education beyond the traditional school years is a must. For the church to stand still while the rest of the world moves on is to court failure. To find new and better ways of discovering and developing its leaders is not merely optional; rather, it is an imperative necessity.

Changing Times Call for Changed Ways

Not long ago, central and regional "training schools" attracted great crowds of church members to study a wide range of textbooks and listen to inspirational addresses. As such occasions waned in popularity, the "conference" was developed. This was an effort to relate the textbooks and the lectures more closely to actual church situations. Recognizing the increasing difficulty of maintaining attendance at interchurch leadership studies, many churches have concentrated their efforts on classes conducted locally. Even so, today's invitation to join a group for the study of a book often does not meet with as enthusiastic a response as formerly

How account for the change? Life has become more crowded and its pace swifter. Other attractive agencies compete for leisure time—radio, television, newspapers, magazines, community affairs, clubs and civic organizations, sports and amusements, travel. Vocational and avocational courses of study are offered by high schools, colleges, and other educational institutions. An increasing number of adult students are enrolling. Public schools make heavier and heavier demands, leaving children and young people little time for other interests.

Individual and group study.—Study of books at home presents an alternative to group study. A planned course of such study, leading to the several awards, may be offered and promoted. Since reading, to have practical educational value, must have guidance, the correspondence course has been found useful.

Along with the text or texts, suggestions are made for problem-solving reading, applying what is read to the local situation. Forms will be filled out indicating the student's reaction and progress. The conscientious and serious student may obtain much value from this type of learning exercise.

However, individual and correspondence study lacks the

important element of group participation. A textbook may inform and stimulate the reader, the correspondence director may ask questions and guide the search for answers, but neither can provide the give-and-take of the leader-group situation. In dialogue, mind reacts to mind, ideas beget ideas, experience adds to experience, resources are combined to find solutions to problems.

In *The Miracle of Dialogue,* Reuel Howe writes: "It [dialogue] can bring relationship into being, and it can bring into being a relationship that has died." He points out that in creative Christian dialogue another person (Jesus Christ) keeps his promise to be present and the miracle of guidance through him and the Holy Spirit takes place. Instead of the group's being the sum total of those present it becomes a vital unity, with insights no one of its members alone could possess.

The "clinic" for problem-solving.—The "clinic" type of leadership education affords this kind of creative experience. The word originally connoted the instructions given by the physician to the patient at the bedside. Then a gathering of medical specialists studied the patient's symptoms and, after joint consultation, prescribed.

Transferred to a church situation, the clinic refers to the bringing together of specialists in various aspects of church life and work who will deal not so much with the textbook itself as its application to actual situations. The superior values of the clinic are obvious. Textbooks are used but they "come alive" as they serve to give guidance to the meeting of real needs in life situations.

The workshop to get results.—This method is a variation of the clinic. As a rule, it is designed for leaders in an actual situation. *Work* signifies effort to attain an objective; *shop,* a place where workmen carry on their occupation or tradesmen their trade. In a workshop, the workmen not only talk about the job but they get it done. Paul F. Douglas says that the purpose of the workshop is to "give people a chance to put their hearts and efforts as equals together in the doing of something worthwhile."

The workshop procedure is relatively simple. Something needs considering and doing: the church calendar revised; the church budget agreed on; an enlargement and enlistment program proposed; teaching and training procedures improved; worship services enriched and attendance increased; community service and social action outlined; missions and evangelism vitalized; solutions to fellowship problems sought; coordination and correlation of activities worked out; team spirit of the church enhanced; a comprehensive program of leadership recruitment and training instigated.

Resources and experiences of the group are brought to bear on the need and its fulfilment. Areas of responsibility are allocated so as to avoid overlapping and misunderstanding.

If needed, reports will be made to the church as a whole for confirmation and action. Decisions reached and plans thus made will have far greater chance of being carried out than if determined by the leader and announced to the group.

Discussion to share ideas.—The discussion method is valuable for leadership training. Actually, it is not so much a method as a principle of method. Concerning almost any important proposal relating to the work of the church, there may be differences of opinion.

The disagreement may be ignored; it may be arbitrarily disposed of by the leader; it may be debated and decided by majority vote; the decision may rankle in the minds and hearts of the dissidents and crop up to cause trouble later. Obviously, none of these ways is satisfactory.

In a free society, permanent resolution of disagreement is best reached by discussion. If sound procedures are followed, both leader and group will gain valuable experience and reach profitable conclusions through use of the discussion method.

The method involves: (1) a leader who directs the discussion but refuses to dominate or be partisan; (2) participants who observe the rules of Christian decorum and seek light rather than to engender heat; (3) a proposal clearly stated with equally clear statement of contrary views; (4) the objective of discussion clearly understood; (5) viewpoints freely expressed, backed by experience and sound logic; (6) alternatives fairly stated and restated as the discussion proceeds, not for the sake of argument, but in the interest of the church and the cause of Christ; (7) conclusion reached by majority agreement of the group, summed up but not imposed by the leader, and with due respect for those who have not been fully convinced, if there are any.

Discussion according to these guidelines will have educative value for leader and group. Too, it usually leads to decision and action with no damaging aftermath. Those who become skilled in the use of the discussion method will then be able to utilize it in other group meetings when they are called upon to lead.

Role-playing to personalize the difficulty.—The method of role-playing may be profitably and interestingly employed. For instance, in confronting a problematical issue, members of the group might be asked, "What would you do in the situation if you were the involved person?"—perhaps pastor, Sunday School superintendent, Training Union director, or some other officer or committee chairman or a dissatisfied member or critical outsider. Each one assigned a part will act it out as realistically as possible.

For example, suppose the problem is one of procedure. The question is raised: What steps would you take if you had this responsibility?

Persons who never really before faced the actual difficulties of a job may now see them in a different light as they try to play the role. The problem may be that of relationships—leader to group, teacher to class, member to member, group to group.

The leader or teacher presides, while selected members act out the difficulty and arrive at conclusions which they think would improve relationships.

Preparation for visitation and personal Christian witnessing may be made through role-playing. The visitor or witness will make an approach to a selected member of the group; the two will carry on a conversation much as if it were in an actual situation. Objections will be raised and answers made, difficulties will be stated and suggestions given as to how they may be overcome.

What happens if the venture fails? What next if it succeeds? In review, the leader will evaluate strong and weak points of the discussion and thus develop confidence and skill when the actual experience occurs.

Roger Bellows, in *Creative Leadership,* says that "role-playing is designed to provide concrete, down-to-earth, true-to-life experiences in which both the trainee and the trainer are interested. Alternate solutions to problems arising from such experiences can be revealed through this technique. Both the trainer and the members of the group interact with a common set toward the material being role-played."

Apprenticeship to learn from association.—The observation-apprenticeship method of leadership-learning may prove useful. The in-service leader who has had limited experience may, with much profit, observe other leaders in similar situations.

He may justifiably have himself excused from his responsibility for a time in order that he may visit other churches to see how leaders are doing their work. From this observation he may learn both positive and negative lessons—how to do his job better and how not to do it.

The in-training leader may form a copartnership with someone already in the position for which he is preparing. At times he will observe but occasionally he will take over while the regular leader watches and then shares with constructive criticism.

The apprenticeship method is one of the oldest means by which a novice in a trade is brought to the level of master. Jesus used this method in training the twelve and the seventy. He instructed them; they observed him in action and then went out on their own to get experience. He praised and corrected them when they returned. Earnest and willing learners thus trained will almost certainly make good leaders.

Dramatization to make the situation "come alive."— The dramatic method, although exacting, may be productive of leaders. The drama has been called "truth or fiction in action." It differs from role-playing in that a story, true or fictional, is enacted. A cast of characters play the several parts.

In medieval Europe, religious plays were popular, such as the Punch-and-Judy (Pontius Pilate and Judas) shows and the Passion plays, reenacting the suffering, death, and resurrection of Christ. Later, theatricals fell into disrepute because of abuses; now television and the movies have brought the theater into homes and communities with powerful influence, whether for good or evil.

Under skilled guidance, the use of carefully selected motion pictures and the presentation of wholesome plays may discover and develop leadership that finds expression in many ways.

The project to learn by doing.—The "project method"

combines many values for leadership education. It is based on the simple principle of "learning by doing." It is especially useful in developing leadership for community service. "Be ye doers of the word, and not hearers only," James, the practical apostle, warns (1:22). Jesus pictured the man who built his house to withstand the storm as the one "who hears these words of mine and does them" (Matt. 7:24).

There are many community services that church groups can render: to prisoners in penal institutions, to the sick in hospitals, to children in orphanages, to residents in homes for the aged, to the underprivileged in slum areas, to neglected members of minority races.

There are community causes that need fostering: better schools, better libraries, better housing, better health conditions, better race relations, better homes.

There are persons to be reached who cannot or will not attend the regular church services: shut-ins who are ill, shut-outs who have to work Sundays, unchurched who can be reached through a mission, untaught who can be led to Bible study in neighborhood home classes, unsaved who can be visited and won to Christ where they are.

In carrying out such projects, leaders are often discovered in unexpected places. As a result, they and the church are enriched.

Variation of Methods

Of these several methods, which may be considered best? The answer will depend largely on the church—its stage of development; its size and leadership resources; its location and transportation facilities; its spirit of unity and progress; its evangelistic and missionary zeal; its commitment to sacrificial service and witness at home and abroad.

Experience indicates that the best beginning point is the well-planned use of church study course textbooks, promoted consistently for individuals or local church groups and on an area-wide basis for cooperating churches. Clearly, however, there is need for supplemental plans according to suggestions outlined above, with combinations and modifications appropriate to the local situation.

The poorest method would be the exclusive use of any one of these! Paul admonished, "Test everything; hold fast what is good" (1 Thess. 5:21). Jesus proposed the ultimate test: "So, every sound tree bears good fruit, but the bad tree bears evil fruit. . . . Thus you will know them by their fruits" (Matt. 7:17-20).

Key persons in any fruitful church leadership program are pastor, staff members, and heads of the several organizations and their associates. Their most rewarding service in the extension and improvement of leadership is in a supervisory capacity.

Sound supervision involves certain essentials: (1) a supervisor who is well acquainted with the task to be done; (2) friendly relations between the supervisor and those whom he would help; (3) understanding of the purpose of supervision—not criticism but helpful consultation; (4) observation of the supervised leader in action; (5) mental notes made by the supervisor of strong and weak points of the supervised leader; (6) constructive conversation with the person thus observed as to weak and strong points, with major emphasis on positive elements; (7) and cooperatively planned improvement measures.

What better service can the pastor as chief of staff and his lieutenants render than this constructive help to those who need it in the betterment of their leadership? Supervision must never be interpreted as "snoopervision" but rather as "friendship with a purpose."

The "population explosion" has immensely increased the opportunity and responsibility of most churches. The unreached multitudes steadily outrun the typical church's leadership personnel with which to find them, proclaim to them and educate them, and win them to Christ and enlist them for service.

On the average, for every ten additional persons reached there must be at least one more person in a position of leadership.

Where are they coming from? "Not from the clouds but from the crowds." The church's outreach and effectiveness, therefore, depend largely on discovering, recruiting, and developing potential leaders.

In every church there are members who could serve in positions of leadership if attractively invited and given needed pretraining. With church approval and under competent guidance, a special class or unit may be formed in which are enrolled carefully selected persons with leadership possibilities who are not now in service.

The group may well be a specialized unit of Training Union. Meeting weekly at a convenient time—perhaps Sunday evening —the future leaders' class will continue for one or two quarters, its primary purpose being to acquaint its members with the leadership needs of the church and qualifications for and responsibilities of the several positions to be filled.

Resource persons from the several church organizations may be brought in to present needs and duties and the appeal for help. On occasion, members of the group may serve as supply for absentee workers, thus getting actual experience in the place of their choice. The church's nominating committee will in this way be supplied with names of persons who have enough familiarity with the places to be filled to reduce to a minimum refusals to serve and risk of failure through lack of preparation.

Continued year by year, this plan should provide a church with a supply of capable persons from which to draw its needed leaders to expand and improve all its services.

A Church's Christlike Investment

A church may make many investments, but it is doubtful if any will return so great dividends as the provision and promotion of full and varied opportunities for leadership recruitment and training. To major on this investment is no longer optional, if ever it was. A church cannot rise higher than its leadership and its leaders cannot go much further than their preparation affords. The church that considers it a minor matter to equip its leaders and enlarge their numbers will default on its commission from its commander and its obligation to itself, its community, and the world.

Jesus Christ recognized this truth when he inaugurated his redemptive mission. Immediately following the announcement of his purpose, he began to recruit men whom he would train for leadership. He preached, he taught, he healed, he evangelized. But he did all in the presence of these men who were thus being trained to follow his example.

In his fervent intercession just before going to the cross, with the disciples at the center of his concern, Jesus prayed: "As thou didst send me into the world, so I have sent them into the world" (John 17:18). He did not send them out unprepared, for he had given more of his precious time to their training than to any other single thing.

Something to Think and Pray About

Why should education continue throughout the whole of life? What is the significance for the church of the adult education movement?

Have we enough leaders (servants of the church) to meet our needs and fulfil our obligations?

Have we an adequate plan for recruiting and training future leaders?

What opportunities do we afford for the fullest development of those whom the church calls into its service?

Are these opportunities sufficiently attractive and varied to equip for greatest effectiveness our present and future leaders?

Of the leadership education methods described above, which are we using? Which are we neglecting?

Are pastor and staff, deacons and church officers, heads of departments and their assistants ready and willing to institute a broader and more varied program of leadership recruitment and training?

If the church is negligent to provide new and better ways of training for present and future leaders, what will be the consequences?

8 The Costs and the Rewards

"What's the price?" the customer asks the salesperson. When told, the prospective purchaser asks himself: Is the price too high? Is it worth what it costs? Can I afford it?

The seller asks: How much profit will I make? How can I induce the customer to buy?

These are legitimate questions in our free-enterprise economy. The buyer wants as much as he can get for his money; the seller wants as much profit as the traffic will properly bear.

In the field of Christian service, the leader has the right to ask, What are the costs and rewards?

And the church may well ask, What inducements can we offer that will enlist sufficient workers for the tasks?

One who holds or contemplates accepting church responsibility should be aware that leadership involves hazards and temptations.

James warns that "we who teach shall be judged with greater strictness" (3:1). The leader is more noticed than others, has more influence, and is more subject to criticism than others. Therefore, he must watch his step with greater care.

There is the danger of pride of position. Election to church office does not confer personal superiority. Jesus warned against pride of office, saying, "But you are not to be called rabbi, for you have one teacher, and you are all brethren" (Matt. 23:8). It is easy for the leader to fall into the error of exalting himself because he holds an important office. Pride is a cardinal sin, often unrecognized and, therefore, all the more dangerous.

The leader may be tempted to further his own interests. Because of his position, he may think of himself as a privileged person. Consciously or unconsciously, he may use his place in the church for self-regarding purposes. Judas is an extreme example—he used his place among the twelve as a means of getting money. Jesus says that, "from within, out of the heart of man, come evil thoughts" (Mark 7:21). The Christian leader must be constantly on guard lest he be found using his church position for selfish ends.

The church leader may develop authoritarianism. The "will to power" is inherent in men. Any position of responsibility carries with it a certain amount of authority. The danger is that this sense of authority may lead to the desire to dominate. The "church boss" is a well-known figure, recognized by others but seldom by "the boss" himself.

Jesus condemned this love of place and power, directing his scorn to the Pharisees who, he said, "love the place of honor at feasts and the best seats in the synagogues, and salutations in the market places, and being called rabbi by men" (Matt. 23:6-7). He concluded, "Whoever exalts himself will be humbled, and whoever humbles himself will be exalted" (v. 12). The leader who loves power may get it, but he will lose the commendation of Christ and ultimately the respect of his fellow Christians.

Always there is danger of insincerity. The image of the church leader is properly that of the good man, sincere and upright, living what he professes to be. Notwithstanding this expectation of him, the leader may be tempted to act otherwise at home, in business, in politics, in social affairs. Such behavior may reach the point that it deserves the denunciation of Jesus: "Woe to you, . . . for you are like whitewashed tombs, which outwardly appear beautiful, but within they are full of dead men's bones and all uncleanness" (Matt. 23:27). The leader whom this describes will destroy himself.

The leader may be tempted to jealousy. Jealousy arises when one's prestige is threatened by another. It is not easy to see another receive the praise and honor which one desires for oneself. The tendency is to discredit the object of jealousy. All sorts of excuses may be invented to justify the jealous attitude. Unchecked, it will spoil usefulness and happiness.

Even if there be apparent justification for animosity toward the offending person, the injunction of Jesus applies: "Love your enemies and pray for those who persecute you, so that you may be sons of your Father who is in heaven" (Matt. 5:44-45). Disobedience to this command will poison life.

Leadership responsibility carries with it the hazard of anxiety. Looking ahead and planning for the future are marks of good leadership, but if this is accompanied by fear and worry it becomes weakness. The burden of leadership is often more than one can bear alone, but always there is recourse in the one who stands beside—the Holy Spirit. To leave him out of account is to grieve him and to forfeit strength and courage, peace and poise.

Ever present is the danger of doubt. A student said to his teacher, when doubt was being discussed, "I have never had a doubt." The professor replied, "Then you've probably never had a thought!"

Doubt is the gap between a question and its answer. In this sense, doubt is a part of the thought process. One who has all the answers at his fingertips is seldom right.

Doubt is resolved by defining the difficulty; examining possible solutions; from reason and experience and revelation, selecting the solution that seems best and then trying it out to confirm its correctness.

Religious doubt has its answer in faith at work. Jesus said, "If any man's will is to do his will, he shall know" (John 7:17). To doubt and do nothing about it, to let doubt become chronic, brings leadership paralysis.

The Initial Cost: Full Commitment

The entrance requirement of Christian leadership is full commitment. If this price is not paid, leadership will go limping. Halfheartedness in any endeavor brings eventual failure. Some nominal church leaders give leftovers of time and energy to the task. They may be unwilling to give their best, yet unwilling to give up the place to others. They not only stunt their own growth but stand in the way of those for whom they have accepted responsibility. The Bible is very clear in its rejection of such divided loyalty.

Jesus left no doubt of his call to full commitment: "No one," he declared, "can serve two masters" (Matt. 6:24). "Not every one who says to me, 'Lord, Lord,' shall enter the kingdom of heaven, but he who does the will of my Father" (Matt. 7:21). Jesus said to the seeking young ruler, "Go, sell what you possess and give to the poor, . . . and come, follow me" (Matt. 19:21).

Christ in Gethsemane made the full commitment: "My Father, if it be possible, let this cup pass from me; nevertheless, not as I will, but as thou wilt" (Matt. 26:39).

Threatened with dire punishment if they did not cease their witness for Christ, Peter and John replied, "Whether it is right in the sight of God to listen to you rather than to God, you must judge; for we cannot but speak of what we have seen and heard" (Acts 4:19-20). In the face of certain death, Stephen preached Christ.

The record continues through Christian history—leaders for Christ have been willing to pay the price of complete commitment for his sake. Leadership for him cannot attain its full measure without this spirit of self-surrender.

The Personal Cost: Sacrifice

Jesus spoke plainly of those who could not be his disciples. He said to the men whom he was calling into his service: "He who loves father or mother more than me is not worthy of me; and he who loves son or daughter more than me is not worthy of me; and he who does not take his cross and follow me is not worthy of me" (Matt. 10:37-38).

Again he said: "Whoever does not bear his own cross and come after me, cannot be my disciple" (Luke 14:27). To the two men who were undecided and wanted to delay making their commitment, Jesus said, "No one who puts his hand to the plow and looks back is fit for the kingdom of God" (Luke 9:62). When he sent the seventy out on their mission, he said, "I send you out as lambs in the midst of wolves" (Luke 10:3).

Just before his crucifixion, Jesus warned the twelve, "They will deliver you up to councils; and you will be beaten in synagogues; and you will stand before governors and kings for my sake, to bear testimony before them" (Mark 13:9). Of the converted and commissioned Saul (Paul), the risen Christ said, "I will show him how much he must suffer for the sake of my name" (Acts 9:16). Recounting the price he paid for his Christian leadership, Paul wrote of afflictions, hardships, calamities, beatings, imprisonments, tumults, labors, watching, hunger (2 Cor. 6:4-5).

In the General Epistles and the Revelation, endurance of

suffering even to death is described as the mark of the Christian. One cannot read the New Testament and doubt that the way of Christian discipleship and leadership is the way of the cross. Rather than a deterrent, this challenge of the difficult has brought to the service of Christ, and his church, leaders of the highest order.

The Intangible Cost: Dedication

Fortunately, religious persecution has ended in all but a few distant parts of the world. Does this mean that now leadership for Christ has become easy? Or is the cost of a different kind but just as real?

Christian leadership costs sweat of brain. Bible study involves far more than a casual reading of the text. The Bible was written in other eras, in other languages, in thought forms different from those with which we are now familiar. It is a progressive revelation. God revealed himself and his purposes as the people were able to receive and understand his disclosures.

The Bible is relevant to life today, but its application requires interpretation. Whatever the leader's position, he needs to relate it to the biblical revelation; and to do so requires continuous Bible study. In addition, there is need of concentrated study of available materials and helps related to the job. No serious Christian leader is exempt from continuous study.

Christian leadership costs self-discipline. Always the temptation is to take the easy way. Self-denial in the New Testament sense means saying no to self and yes to Christ. Sacrifice is not doing something burdensome and distasteful but gladly devoting one's best to that which is greater than self. Make no mistake—such self-discipline is the "narrow way" and is not easy to travel.

The Christian leader's dedication involves the sort of mastery over self which Paul described: "I pommel my body and subdue it, lest after preaching to others I myself should be disqualified" (1 Cor. 9:27).

Christian leadership costs the practice of prayer. Prayer is far more than repetition of familiar words. Prayer stems from concern that calls for divine help to meet the need. Prayer is bringing to God the leader's problems and listening to him for solutions. Prayer is intercession for troubled persons who must have more than human help. Prayer is costly, for one who prays thus must be willing to serve as God's instrument in answering the prayer.

The Tangible Cost: Time and Money

Christian leadership costs time and energy. "Dost thou love life? Then do not squander time, for that is the stuff life is made of," said Poor Richard (Benjamin Franklin). Each one of us has just so much time and no more. In the budgeting of time, the Christian leader must firmly set aside that regular portion demanded for the worthy performance of his job. Time and energy are closely related. Again, each one has a limited quota of energy. If it is expended in one direction, it cannot be used in another. Worthy Christian service demands that a worthy proportion of energy be reserved for the task.

Christian leadership costs money. Money, too, is life transmuted into currency. In a money-centered economy, its use becomes a test of devotion and loyalty. Christian stewardship is a recognition of God's claim on a proportion of one's income (normally one tenth) which belongs to God and is to be used under the will of the owner for the purposes of Jesus Christ. The Christian leader is under obligation to set an example of stewardship of money as well as of all the rest of life.

The Prize: Growth

The human tragedy is failure to grow. The baby that remains a baby to the end of life brings a sense of despair to the parents. The adult who continues to behave as a child mars his own happiness and that of others. The empty life that grows steadily emptier has "missed the mark" and become a failure. The twisted, malformed, rebellious personality is headed for disaster and is a menace to society. The high prize of life is to grow as Jesus did—"in wisdom and in stature, and in favor with God and man" (Luke 2:52).

Personality attains its maximum potential through processes of growth. Personality growth is not apart from tensions. Tension arises when there is a gap between effort and goal. One may abandon the effort, lower the aim, or follow Paul's example and "press on toward the goal for the prize of the upward call of God in Christ Jesus" (Phil. 3:14). If effort slackens or the prize is abandoned, life becomes static and personality deteriorates. The Christian leader leads by what he is and by what he is becoming. He must meet the conditions of continuous growth.

Socrates summed up the human imperative in two words, "Know thyself." Tennyson wrote: "Self-reverence, self-knowledge, self-control, these . . . lead life to sovereign power."

The basic determinants of selfhood are heredity, environment, history, choice, providence. No one can entirely escape the influence of heritage; the surroundings in which one is born and grows up powerfully shape personality; the records bequeathed by one's ancestry become a part of one's life; personal decisions enter into the very warp and woof of one's being.

Shakespeare said, "There's a divinity that shapes our ends, rough-hew them as we will." To understand oneself requires frequent review of these intermingled factors. Each one plays a part in determining personality.

The way of growth is understanding others. The leader will ask concerning each one in his class or group: What has this individual in common with other group members? What are some distinctive differences? How account for his or her responses? What needs are apparent? How can these needs be met? If unsaved, how can this person be led to Christ? If a Christian, how can character be developed and strengthened? The leader will find himself growing as he helps others to grow.

The leader will be called on to cultivate compassion. When Jesus looked on the crowds about him, "he had compassion for them, because they were harassed and helpless, like sheep without a shepherd" (Matt. 9:36). Compassion is a strong word, denoting more than pity or sympathy. To have compassion is to put oneself in the place of others, to suffer with them, to be moved by their needy condition.

The compassion of Jesus led him to do something about it. He called his disciples about him, instructed them, and sent them out to "heal the sick, raise the dead, cleanse lepers, cast out demons" (Matt. 10:8). Such ministries called for deep compassion; and the disciples grew in compassion as they obeyed the commission and followed the example of their compassionate Lord.

The Christian leader who thus serves human need grows that tenderness of heart which becomes a priceless ingredient of happiness.

The way of growth is the way of renunciation. Jesus stated the profound life principle: "Whoever would save his life will lose it, and whoever loses his life for my sake will find it" (Matt. 16:25). This requires the choice of higher values in the presence of lower.

Many calls for investment of life come from many directions. What will lead on to an ever-expanding life? What choice will narrow and eventually destroy life? The answer is clear: the high choice is to lose one's life in the self-forgetting service of others for Christ's sake. This is the sure way of growth toward and to the best in life.

The way of growth is the unending quest for competency. The leader must realize that whatever he does can be done better. Jesus set the standard high: "You, therefore, must be perfect, as your heavenly Father is perfect" (Matt. 5:48).

Like the horizon, this ideal recedes as it is approached. Paul felt this urge toward unattained perfection: "Not that I have already obtained this or am already perfect; but I press on to make it my own, because Christ Jesus has made me his own" (Phil. 3:12).

Browning said that "a man's reach should exceed his grasp, or what's a heaven for?" Here is a paradox: dissatisfaction with achievement leads to greater achievement; discontent with personal growth leads to more growth. Life becomes more worthwhile to him who is ever striving to attain greater heights.

The Reward: Life Enrichment

Jesus said, "I came that they may have life, and have it abundantly" (John 10:10). The abundant life is both a bestowment and an achievement. It cannot be had apart from Christ; yet he does not bestow it apart from deserving. Salvation is a gift, but the rewards of the saved life are earned. The Christian leader is especially blessed in the privileges afforded for the enrichment of life—his own and others.

The leader's reward is enrichment of knowledge. The preacher learns more of theology and the gospel than do those to whom he preaches. The deacon or church officer learns more about ecclesiology and church polity than do those whom he serves. Sunday School officers and teachers learn more about the Bible than do class members. The leader of a service organization learns better how to serve than those who sit on the sidelines. The music director gains a greater mastery of church music than those who are directed. Leaders are called on to give more, but they get more.

The leader's reward is enrichment of understanding of others. The true leader is more concerned about others than himself. He realizes that every person is unique—in all the world there are no two persons exactly alike. He understands that each person is a universe of possibilities, yet these potentialities cannot be actualized apart from interaction with other persons.

Any class or group, however large or small, furnishes the leader a limitless laboratory for research.

What are each member's peculiarities? What has this individual in common with other members? How and why does each one characteristically respond? What are distinctive abilities, needs, resources? What will be the best approach to lead to Christ or to deeper devotion?

Answers to such questions, through conversation and companionship, will enrich the life of the leader and of each one whom he seeks to serve.

The leader is enriched by love. Beyond any accumulation of wealth, any possession of power, any satisfaction of desire, is the power to love and the reward of being loved. To love and and to be loved are not automatic responses. One must learn the art of loving and be worthy of being loved. Christian love is self-giving on behalf of another. Christian love is to love the unlovely as well as the lovely. The poorest man is the loveless, the richest man the one most loved.

Love asks nothing in return but the privilege of loving. There is a key that can unlock the door to love in the hardest heart. The Christian leader's search is for the key until he finds it. In the quest and discovery, the leader learns the art of loving and earns the love of others in return. What richer prize at the end of the journey than to have it said, "He loved us and we loved him"?

The leader is enriched by steadfast loyalty to high purpose. The aimless life is the empty life. Many let the years come and go with no higher purpose than to eat and sleep, to work and play, to satisfy their temporal needs and appease their sensual appetites. For them, life in the closing years is like a shriveled apple with a worm at the core. Visit a home for the aged or a community of retired senior citizens and observe the two groups —those who have lived purposefully and have maintained their zest for life and those who have lived without high purpose and have nothing left to live for, even though they may have enough to live on. The useful leader's joy is to be like the sound apple, mellowest and sweetest as it gets ready to fall from the bough.

The most precious enrichment of the leader is the sense of God's approval, of Christ's presence, and the Holy Spirit's guidance and comfort. The servant of the Word has learned that he cannot do it alone and that he does not have to. He knows that he is never alone and that even his failures can be turned to good account by his divine comrades and helpers.

When under criticism—and this is often the lot of the leader —he may ask with Paul: "Who shall bring any charge against God's elect? . . . Who shall separate us from the love of Christ?" (Rom. 8:33-35). The answer: "It is God who justifies" (v. 33). "In all these things we are more than conquerors through him who loved us" (v. 37).

The Satisfaction: Worthwhileness

There is the satisfaction of usefulness. Emptiness of life usually comes from a sense of uselessness. Happiness is serving others without expectation of pay. In the parable of the talents, the two servants were called blessed who did the best they could with what they had; the wrong of the condemned servant was that he did nothing. The leader's good fortune is that he is privileged above others to be useful.

The compensation for faithful discharge of responsibility is more responsibility. Perhaps you have said, "The more I do, the more I am expected to do." Good! You are being rewarded. In the parable of the pounds the man who doubled the money entrusted to him was not retired on a pension—he was made ruler over ten cities. Achievement is not an end in itself, it is rather a step toward greater achievement. The life worthwhile is not static but expanding. The joy of the leader is to have the confidence of friends who expect of him more and more.

The reward of the leader is an exhilarating sense of significance. This is not egotism, which is self-centeredness. To be significant is to feel that one's life counts not for self but for others. Men undergo "toil, sweat, and tears" if they believe sufficiently that it makes a difference. Christian leadership, even in a minor position, brings this high satisfaction.

The satisfaction of leadership is a developing creativity. Life for many tends to get in a rut. "Life is so daily," they complain. To be in Christ is to be "a new creation," with exciting possibilities and a fresh outlook even on commonplace duties. Companionship with other like-minded Christians and the privilege of winning others to Christ and to his service stimulate to new ways of thinking and acting that constitute one of life's keenest pleasures.

Measureless is the satisfaction of appreciation and gratitude. To have someone say sincerely, "I appreciate what you are doing," or, "You have helped me and I thank you" makes the effort worth all it costs—and more. Even though the words are unspoken, appreciation and gratitude may be sensed and the leader's heart warmed beyond anything that material success could bring.

Pay the Price—Receive the Reward

Even more gratifying than man's approval is Christ's approval: "Well done, good and faithful servant; . . . enter into the joy of your master" (Matt. 25:21). This reward has in it the quality of eternity, for in the judgment it will bring the welcome of Christ the Judge, "Come, O blessed of my Father, inherit the kingdom prepared for you from the foundation of the world" (v. 34).

Count the cost, Jesus warns. Pay the price and reap reward, he challenges. Even the cup of cold water given in his name will be rewarded, he assures. The life lost in his service will be saved, he guarantees. The greatest leader is the servant of all, he declares. "Be faithful unto death," he pledges, "and I will give you the crown of life" (Rev. 2:10).

Whatever the costs, we conclude, they will be outweighed by the rewards. Trust him for the outcome, follow where he leads, and grace, mercy, and peace from the Triune God will be yours. Attributed to Elizabeth Barrett Browning is this conclusion:

> The sweetest lives are those to duty wed,
>   Whose deeds, both great and small,
> Are close-knit strands of unbroken thread
>   Where love ennobles all.
>
> The world may sound no trumpets, ring no bells;
> The book of life the shining record tells.
>
>   .   .   .   .
>
> Thou shalt be served thyself by every sense
> Of service which thou renderest.

Something to Think and Pray About

Is it right for the individual and the church to raise the question as to costs and rewards of Christian leadership?

Do the demands which Jesus made for discipleship help or hinder in the call to Christian leadership?

Of the hazards and temptations that inhere in leadership, which concerns you most? What resources do you depend on to meet and overcome them?

Is your commitment to your church responsibility wholehearted and unreserved? If not, how can it be made so?

Are you growing satisfyingly as a Christian and church worker? What rewards of continuing growth are you seeking?

What enrichments are your church duties and relationships bringing? How can this enrichment be increased?

Do you deserve the rewards that Jesus has promised to those who serve him and his church faithfully? Ask yourself, "What lack I yet?" Then decide how this lack may be supplied.

A Self-Rating Scale for Leaders and Prospective Leaders

Check under YES, NO, TO SOME EXTENT the answer concerning yourself that seems to you most nearly correct.

	YES	NO	TO SOME EXTENT
1. I am aware of the urgent need of more and better leaders.	——	——	——
2. I agree with the statement that I can learn to lead.	——	——	——
3. I agree that I am needed to lead.	——	——	——
4. I think I have a satisfactory concept of leadership.	——	——	——
5. I believe that Christian leadership extends to Christian social action.	——	——	——
6. I realize that my church needs me for some special service.	——	——	——
7. My orginal concept of the leader did not extend to average, unexceptional persons.	——	——	——
8. I now accept Jesus' revolutionary teaching concerning leadership.	——	——	——

9. I am willing to be guided by this radical leadership ideal.

10. I understand how, historically, the New Testament leadership ideal became secularized.

11. I recognize that the secular concept of leadership has infiltrated today's churches.

12. I can describe ways in which the servantship ideal of leadership is being imperiled.

13. I am willing to commit myself to the servantship ideal of leadership.

14. Checking my leadership qualifications (p. 40), I find that my strong points outweigh my weak points.

15. My weak points will not automatically bar me from accepting leadership responsibility.

16. My weaknesses are shared by others and can be overcome.

17. Adopting the servantship viewpoint would go far toward solving our church's leadership problem.

18. Progress in any endeavor requires planning.

19. Effective leadership requires continuous preparation.

20. I seek divine guidance in my leadership preparation.

21. I make use of the best available printed helps.

22. I am familiar with my denomination's plan for leadership training. ___ ___ ___

23. I expect to follow consecutive steps of study leading to increasingly higher awards. ___ ___ ___

24. I favor correlating the several church organizations for cooperative leadership training. ___ ___ ___

25. I recognize that faithful study and practice of church leadership will prepare me for other duties. ___ ___ ___

26. I need to know more exactly the job I now hold or may hold in the church. ___ ___ ___

27. I believe I can define accurately the objective of my church responsibility. ___ ___ ___

28. I agree that clear-cut objectives are essential to success in a position of leadership. ___ ___ ___

29. I am conscious that the welfare of persons is a basic aim in Christian leadership. ___ ___ ___

30. I am prepared to reject faulty ways of leading in favor of the Christian principle of shared responsibility. ___ ___ ___

31. I consider myself a loyal member of a cooperating church team. ___ ___ ___

32. I stand ready to give up my way in the interest of the welfare of the church as a whole. ___ ___ ___

33. I have consistently sought accord in my church relations. ___ ___ ___

34. I recognize that "togetherness" is an essential of the church of Jesus' intention.

_____ _____ _____

35. I understand the historical background of independency of the several church organizations.

_____ _____ _____

36. I desire to help bring about a fuller correlation of these organizations.

_____ _____ _____

37. I am determined to help maintain "the unity of the Spirit" in my leadership relations.

_____ _____ _____

38. While adhering to unchanged principles, I am ready to use new methods to meet changed conditions.

_____ _____ _____

39. I would like for our church to try out some of the methods described which we are not now using.

_____ _____ _____

40. I am in favor of instituting a special class or group for pretraining prospective leaders.

_____ _____ _____

41. I am convinced that our church must enlarge its leadership education program if it meets today's demands.

_____ _____ _____

42. I recognize that our church as a whole should accept responsibility for selection and training of its leaders.

_____ _____ _____

43. I understand that Christian leadership involves hazards and hardships.

_____ _____ _____

44. I can locate within myself some of the leadership temptations described in chapter 8.

_____ _____ _____

45. I have found ways to meet and overcome my leadership temptations.

_____ _____ _____

46. So far as in me lies, I am committed to Christ and the leadership responsibility I bear in my church. ___ ___ ___

47. Gratefully I claim the rewards that are mine through faithful Christian service. ___ ___ ___

48. Happily I am ready to pay the price of fulfilment of my Christian leadership duties. ___ ___ ___

49. Confidently I trust the living Christ to be with me as I seek to follow where he leads. ___ ___ ___

50. Expectantly I turn to the Holy Spirit for guidance in all my planning and serving. ___ ___ ___

Rate Yourself

Count the number of times you have checked YES in the first column. This is your POSITIVE SCORE.

Count the number of times you have checked NO in the second column. This is your NEGATIVE SCORE.

Count the number of times you have checked the TO SOME EXTENT column. This is your DOUBTFUL SCORE.

Study your POSITIVE leadership points. How many of them can you sincerely take credit for on your own account? How many of them are due largely to the help and influence of others? How many wholly to the grace and goodness of God? What are your conclusions?

Consider your NEGATIVE leadership points. How many are due to correctable faults of your own? How many are due to the influence of others or to traditions which you have inherited? How many are due to circumstances beyond your control? What do you propose to do about it?

Count the number of times you have checked the TO SOME
EXTENT column. In what way do you think you are justified in
being doubtful about the point? Are you concerned to change
it from DOUBTFUL to YES or NO? Why? What do you conclude?

Let Someone Else Rate You

Ask someone who knows you well and is sympathetic and understanding to rate you on the points in the scale above. How
does this friend's rating compare with yours? How does this
help you to see yourself as others see you? What does it indicate as to your need of improvement for maximum leadership
effectiveness?

Rate Someone Else

Select another person in your leadership group whom you
know quite well; according to your best judgment, rate him or
her on the scale above. How does the outcome compare with
your self-rating and the rating of yourself by another? What
encouragement (or discouragement) does this bring? How can
you help this fellow worker to improve as a leader?

Rate the Church Leadership as a Whole

Admittedly an "educated guess," check the list above, having in
mind the total church leadership (or that within your particular
organization). Does the rating tend to be more positive, negative, or doubtful? What does this indicate as to the need of
discussion, evaluation, determination to capitalize on the strong
points and strengthen the weak points that have been disclosed?
What method would be best suited to this procedure?

Reading for Further Enrichment

Auer, Jeffrey, and Eubank, Henry Lee. *Handbook for Discussion Leaders.* New York: Harper & Bros., 1947.

Aultman, Donald S. *Learning Christian Leadership.* Grand Rapids: Baker Book House, 1960.

Bellows, Roger. *Creative Leadership.* Englewood Cliffs, N. J.: Prentice-Hall, 1959.

Bennett, Thomas R. *The Leader and the Process of Change.* New York: Association Press, 1962.

Blackwood, Andrew W. *Pastoral Leadership.* New York: Abingdon-Cokesbury Press, 1949.

Bradford, Leland, Stock, Dorothy, and Horowitz, Murray. *Understanding How Groups Work.* Chicago: Adult Education Association, 1955.

Brandt, Alvin G. *Drama Handbook for Churches.* New York: Seabury Press, 1964.

Buchanan, Paul C. *The Leader and Individual Motivation.* New York: Association Press, 1962.

Dewey, John. *Democracy and Education.* New York: The Macmillan Co., 1923.

Dobbins, Gaines S. *The Ministering Church.* Nashville: Broadman Press, 1960.

Douglass, Paul F. *The Group Workshop Way in the Church.* New York: Association Press, 1956.

Douty, Mary Alice. *How to Work with Church Groups.* Nashville: Abingdon Press, 1957.

Euting, George L. *The Brotherhood Program of a Baptist Church.* Memphis: Brotherhood Commission, 1966.

FRANK, LAWRENCE K. *How to Be a Modern Leader.* New York: Association Press, 1954.

GORDON, THOMAS. *Group-Centered Leadership.* Boston, Houghton-Mifflin, 1953.

HAIMAN, F. S. *Group Leadership and Democratic Action.* Boston: Houghton-Mifflin, 1951.

HARNER, NEVIN C. *About Myself.* Philadelphia: Christian Education Press, 1950.

HARRELL, JOHN. *Teaching Is Communicating.* New York: Seabury Press, 1965.

HARRIS, PHILIP B. *The Training Program of a Church.* Nashville: Convention Press, 1966.

HART, W. NEILL. *Home and Church Working Together.* Nashville: Abingdon Press, 1951.

HOWE, REUEL L. *The Miracle of Dialogue.* New York: Seabury Press, 1963.

HOWSE, W. L., AND THOMASON, W. O. *A Church Organized and Functioning.* Nashville: Convention Press, 1963.

JONES, IDRIS. *Our Church Plans for Adult Education.* Philadelphia: Judson Press, 1952.

KEISER, ARMILDA. (dramatization) *Here's How and When.* New York: Friendship Press, 1952.

KLEIN, ALAN F. *Role Playing in Leadership Training and Group Problem Solving.* New York: Association Press, 1956.

LINDGREN, HENRY C. *Effective Leadership in Human Relations.* New York: Hermitage House, 1954.

LIPPITT, GORDON L., AND SEASHORE, EDITH. *Leader and Group Effectiveness.* New York: Association Press, 1962.

LITTLE, SARA. *Learning Together in the Christian Fellowship.* Richmond: John Knox Press, 1956.

TEAD, ORDWAY. *The Art of Leadership.* New York: McGraw-Hill Book Co., 1935.

Pamphlets

Adult Education Association of the U.S.A. Chicago: 743 N. Wabash Avenue.
   1. How to Lead Discussions
   2. Planning Better Programs

3. Taking Action in the Community
4. Understanding How Groups Work
5. How to Teach Adults
6. How to Use Role Playing and Other Tools for Learning
7. Supervision and Consultation
8. Training Group Leaders
9. Conducting Workshops and Institutes
10. Conferences That Work

Periodicals

Adult Leadership, published by Adult Leadership Association of the U.S.A., 741 N. Wabash Avenue, Chicago, Ill. (monthly except July-August).

Church Administration, published by Baptist Sunday School Board, 127 Ninth Avenue, N., Nashville, Tenn. (monthly).

The Sunday School Builder, published by Baptist Sunday School Board, 127 Ninth Avenue, N., Nashville, Tenn. (monthly).

The Training Union Magazine, published by Baptist Sunday School Board, 127 Ninth Avenue, N., Nashville, Tenn. (monthly).

Baptist Men's Journal, published by Brotherhood Commission of the Southern Baptist Convention, 1548 Poplar Ave., Memphis, Tenn. (monthly).

The Leader, published by American Baptist Board of Publication, Valley Forge, (monthly).

Religious Education, published by the Religious Education Association, 545 W. 111th Street, New York, N.Y. (bimonthly).